Dinosaur

NATURAL HISTORY MUSEUM

ALIVE

THE STORIES BEHIND THE MUSEUM'S GREAT EXTINCT CREATURES

By Amabel Adcock

Foreword by David Attenborough

With material and images from David Attenborough's Natural History Museum Alive on Sky 3D.
For more information, please visit: www.naturalhistorymuseumalive.com

Dedicated to Rex

Go Entertainment Group
Broadley House, 48 Broadley Terrace
London, NW1 6LG

First published in 2014

Design & Layout: Matt Niblock
Production: Tom James
Foreword © David Attenborough, 2013

Thank you to The Natural History Museum, London for permission to use imagery from their archives.
Also thank you to Getty Images, Corbis, Press Association, Science Photo Library, Royal Geographical
Society, Alexander Turnbull Library, Science Museum / Science & Society Picture Library, Wellesley
Historical Society, Rex Features, Alamy, Dr. Phillip Manning and the artist Joe Venus for providing
images for the book. Illustrations used throughout the book courtesy of Peter Falloon aka The Bear.
CGI images used throughout the book taken from David Attenborough's Natural History Museum Alive.

Colossus Productions: Page 4-5, 6, 15, 16, 17, 18, 19, 23, 24, 25, 26, 27, 29, 35, 38-39, 47, 48, 49,
52, 55, 56-57, 59, 63, 65, 66-67, 69, 74-75, 76, 78, 79, 84, 86-87, 88, 89, 98-99, 105, 106, 107, 108,
109, 110, 111, 112, 113, 114; The Trustees of the Natural History Museum, London: Page 10, 12, 14,
16, 20, 21, 23, 24, 28, 33, 34, 37, 40, 41, 42, 43, 45, 50, 54, 70, 71, 73, 90, 91, 92, 94, 95, 96, 97,
100-101, 103, 104, 105; Michael R Long / The Trustees of the Natural History Museum, London: Page
37, 53; Peter Snowball / The Trustees of the Natural History Museum, London: Page 46; John Sibbick
/ The Trustees of the Natural History Museum, London: Page 61, 80; Florilegius / The Trustees of the
Natural History Museum, London: Page 77, 104; Thom Atkinson / The Trustees of the Natural History
Museum, London: Page 82

GRDBK4953

ISBN: 978-0-9572436-5-1

British Library Cataloguing in Publication Data. A catalogue record for this book is available from the
British Library.

Printed and bound in Poland

CONTENTS

FOREWORD

What did it look like when it was alive? That, I guess, is the first question that comes into most people's minds when they look at the fossilised skeleton of an animal that lived millions of years ago.

The bones usually make clear the general shape of the animal but there are other clues that are less obvious. The shape of the joints between the bones can show how far and in what directions limbs once moved. Scars on the bones can indicate where muscles were once attached and suggest how big, and therefore how powerful, they were. Teeth can tell you what kind of food the animal ate. And once you have worked out what kind of animal it was, you can look at its living relatives to get some idea of how it behaved.

Sometimes the people who first studied the bones will have found answers which everyone agrees are still correct. Sometimes later researchers will have found evidence that show the first conclusions were wrong. And every now and then, it turns out that someone deliberately distorted the evidence in order to make their discoveries seem more impressive.

Recently, Amabel Adcock and a team of experts from London's Natural History Museum reviewed such questions so that we could make a special television programme in 3D. Here are their answers that, with the aid of computers, enabled us to bring to life some of the most important and spectacular animals in the Museum's amazing collections.

David Attenborough

INTRODUCTION TO THE
NATURAL HISTORY MUSEUM, LONDON

The origins of the Natural History Museum's collections are the 80,000 or more specimens amassed by the 18th century collector Sir Hans Sloane. Bought by the nation, they were housed in the British Museum and have been continually added to over the years. Amongst others, they now include specimens collected during such notable expeditions as Captain Cook's epic journey aboard HMS *Endeavour* and the voyages of Charles Darwin on HMS *Beagle*.

By the 1860s, the collections were reaching bursting point and Sir Richard Owen, head of the natural history collections, persuaded the government that a new building was needed. Designed by Alfred Waterhouse, the stunning Romanesque Waterhouse Building was opened to the public in 1881 and this 'Cathedral to Nature' has remained a national treasure ever since.

With more than 80 million specimens, ranging from microscopic slides to mammoth skeletons, the Museum is now home to the largest and most important natural history collection in the world. With approximately 300 scientists working under its roof, it is also one of the largest expert bodies of its kind.

With unprecedented access to these collections and working alongside the Museum's team of scientists, *Natural History Museum Alive 3D* is a unique and groundbreaking project in which some of the Museum's most iconic extinct creatures have been brought back to life with stunning computer-generated imagery, all playing out alongside David Attenborough on the most spectacular of stages, the Natural History Museum, London. This is the story behind these creatures and how they came to be under the guardianship of the Museum.

Profile

Period:
They had become extinct 334 years ago

Habitat:
The lowlands of Mauritius

Size:

HEIGHT
Up to 1 metre (3.3 ft.)

WEIGHT
10–18 kg though most likely at the slimmer end of this scale

Diet:
Its main diet was fallen fruits. With its large beak however, it is possible that it ate nuts, roots or even crustaceans for the calcium.

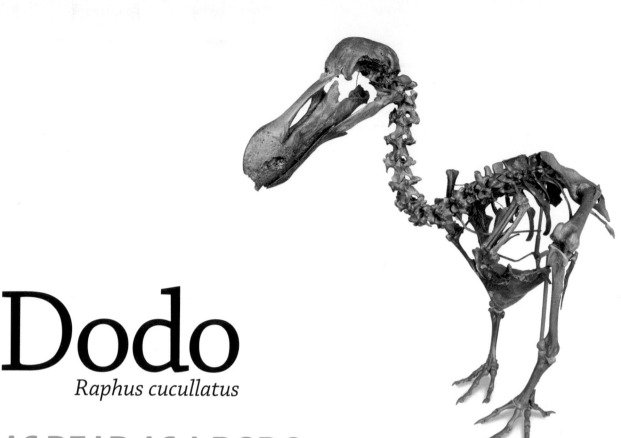

Dodo
Raphus cucullatus

AS DEAD AS A DODO

Perhaps the most famous extinct bird in history and the greatest icon of extinction, the poor old dodo has been resurrected numerous times in popular film and literature. Charles Dodgson (better known by his pen name of Lewis Carroll) was so impressed by the remains of the dodo he observed in the Oxford University Museum of Natural History that it later appeared in his book, *Alice's Adventures in Wonderland*. Illustrations for the book by Sir John Tenniel cemented the dodo as a favourite character in Victorian culture.

Indeed, when it came to deciding which animals should be incorporated into the design of the new Natural History Museum being built in South Kensington, the dodo was one of the obvious choices to represent extinct animals and it can be seen to this day in the panel above a doorway in the Museum's east wing.

Despite its fame, very few people actually observed and recorded the dodo in life, and so it has remained something of a mysterious creature…until now!

◓ *Dodo by Sir John Tenniel in* Alice's Adventures in Wonderland *(Carroll 1865)*

WHERE DID THE DODO LIVE?

The dodo was found only on the island of Mauritius, isolated in the vastness of the Indian Ocean, over 800 kilometres from Madagascar, the nearest landmass. Although Mauritius was probably a regular stopover for Arab traders as early as the thirteenth century, it was not until 1598 that the Dutch East India Company claimed Mauritius as its own and the first settlers arrived. Shortly afterwards records of the flora and fauna of Mauritius began to filter back to Europe and, in particular, reports of a large, clumsy, flightless bird captured people's imaginations.

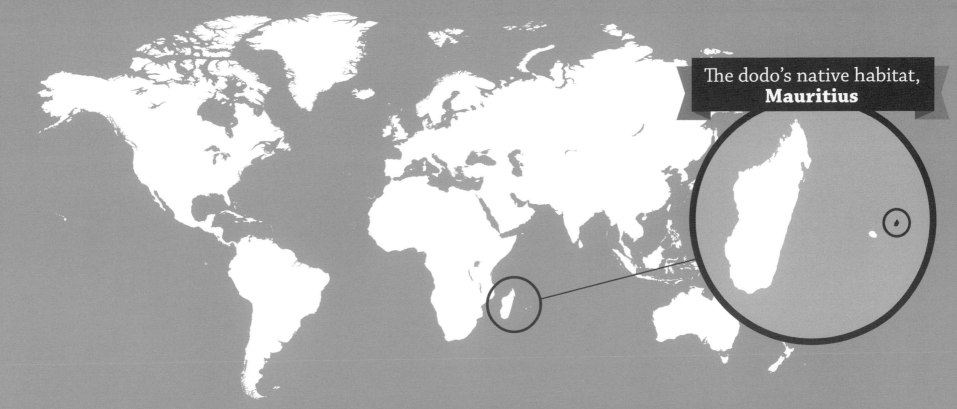

The dodo's native habitat, **Mauritius**

HOW DID THE DODO BECOME EXTINCT?

Within one hundred years of its discovery in 1598, the entire species had become extinct. How? Well, the dodo was probably *not* hunted to extinction by humans as commonly believed. Mariners' reports describe its meat as tough and unpalatable, and the first Dutch settlers even named the bird walckvogel, which literally translates as "disgusting bird". So, rather than being directly exterminated by humans, the dodo was driven to extinction by the animals introduced to Mauritius by human settlers: pigs, goats, rats, monkeys and deer. These animals quickly colonised the island, consuming all the food in their path, including the dodo's eggs which would have lain exposed in shallow nests on the ground.

○ Terracotta moulding of a dodo in the Natural History Museum, London.

◑ 1601 Dutch painting of Mauritius with a walckvogel. Can you spot the dodo?
Credit: Science and Society Picture Library

THE HUNT TO FIND DODO REMAINS

It wasn't until the middle of the nineteenth century that the scientific community became interested in the dodo and, inevitably, a race began to find the first dodo fossil remains. The first bones were discovered by George Clark, who sent them to the two most prominent anatomists of the time – Richard Owen (founder of what is today the Natural History Museum) at the British Museum and Alfred Newton at Cambridge University. However, Owen intercepted the bones intended for Alfred Newton and abused his position at the British Museum to forestall any complaints. Subsequently, Owen was the first person to publish and describe the dodo's anatomy in 1866!

Did You Know?

One theory as to how the dodo got its name, suggests that they made a "doo-doo" cooing noise, not unlike the pigeons they are related to.

● *Dodo model and skeleton, 1938*

WHAT'S IN A NAME?

Scientists at the Natural History Museum have been piecing together the clues to decipher how the dodo got its name. Originally the name was thought to come from the Portuguese word "doudo" meaning foolish or the Dutch word "dodoor" meaning sluggard, words which described the dodo's behaviour from sailors' logs of the time.

● *Nicobar pigeon*

However, DNA analysis has revealed that their closest living relative is in fact a pigeon, the Nicobar pigeon to be precise. So perhaps their name derives from the familiar cooing or "doodoo" noise that a pigeon makes!

WHAT DID THE DODO LOOK LIKE?

Since few complete dodo skeletons have ever been found no one really knew what they looked like. Even the stuffed specimens in the bird gallery of the Natural History Museum are fakes, made using the skeletons and feathers of various birds such as swans and geese, and with plaster beaks, legs and feet.

For centuries, early paintings of the birds have been used as reference for how they looked, but it seems likely these were based on sailors' descriptions rather than being drawn from life. This large, flightless bird, with a hooked beak and bare face and showing no fear of humans, must have caused quite a sensation, and it is not surprising that the birds were depicted as fat, stupid and ungainly looking. The most famous painting of a dodo, and the image that has survived the test of time, was painted by a Dutch artist called Roelandt Savery in 1626.

Over hundreds of years it was this fanciful image of a Dodo that prevailed

In life Savery was rather portly and a confirmed bachelor. Some have interpreted his squat and dumpy image of the dodo to be a self-portrait, juxtaposed with a pair of parrots to emphasise his single status. In the same way, Charles Dodgson wrote himself into *Alice's Adventures in Wonderland* as the dodo, a reference to his stammer and subsequent nickname – Do-Do-Dodgson!

Over hundreds of years it was this fanciful image of a dodo that prevailed, becoming more and more exaggerated with each reconstruction.

ISLAND QUIRKS

The dodo has been accused of being so obese and stupid that it caused its own extinction by being unable to outrun its captors! Well, we now know that these insults were inaccurate – the dodo was neither stupid nor obese – but it was certainly a peculiar looking animal.

As a result of their geographic isolation, islands tend to play host to unusual collections of plants and animals. Just think of the lemurs of Madagascar, the marine iguanas of the Galapagos Islands and the giant moa of New Zealand.

Imagine evolving on an island with virtually no predators and, in particular, with no humans.

Left alone for millions of years, island species sometimes evolve in very different ways. With few predators they can adopt some very strange characteristics, and one of these is flightlessness. With no ground predators, there was no need for the dodo to waste precious energy flying as it could easily find food on foot. Over millions of years its wings became redundant and its body heavier – it no longer needed to be light enough to fly. So rather than being obese, the dodo was in fact large and muscular, perfectly adapted to life on the ground.

Another trait that comes from living in isolation is so-called island tameness. Imagine evolving on an island with virtually no predators and, in particular, no humans. The dodos simply would not have recognised humans as a threat. When the first humans set foot on Mauritius the dodos would have been curious and inquisitive rather than afraid. It is easy to imagine how the dodo gained a reputation for being foolhardy!

PERFECTLY ADAPTED

So if we bring Savery's iconic image of a dodo to life we can begin to see that his depiction is in fact largely inaccurate.

A flightless bird, the dodo would have been large, standing up to a metre in height, and as heavy as a turkey. Analysis of composite skeletons has confirmed that it would have been much slimmer and stood more upright than previously thought.

In fact, rather than being absurdly built, dodos were perfectly adapted for life in the forested lowlands of Mauritius. Their legs would have been strong and robust, capable of bearing their considerable weight. The large openings in the top of the bone at the ankle were for supporting strong tendons attached to large muscles, like a pulley system, to enable the birds to move quickly around despite their great bulk. Their feet were comparatively short – another adaptation to support weight. Their small vestigial wings were weak and useless and could not have supported feathers, but might have been used to balance and steer as they ran through the rocky landscape.

The dodo's diet would have consisted mainly of the fresh, fallen fruit found in abundance across Mauritius, and its bare face would have allowed it to gorge on fruit without getting its feathers in a mess. And what about that large beak? Well, occasionally the dodo would have supplemented its diet with much needed calcium in the form of snail shells, so the large beak was probably needed to crush the hard snail shell.

Did You Know?

The dodo was a large, heavy bird - as big and as weighty as a turkey, weighing up to 18 kilograms. The skeleton of the dodo was actually well structured to support the weight of the bird. As the dodo evolved flightlessness, the bird got heavier and heavier. This can be seen in the robust leg bones, which were designed to support its weight.

Did You Know?

They used their large beak as a weapon during territorial disputes between males. Dodos were almost certainly monogamous, and males would have fought doggedly for females during the breeding season.

A MATE FOR LIFE

SCAN HERE

And what about the colour of their feathers? There have been reports of dodos ranging in colour from browns, to yellows, and even to blue. We know that the dodo was probably a highly monogamous bird like other pigeon species, finding and sticking with a mate for life, so perhaps their facial skin might have changed colour in the breeding season to help them attract the best possible mate?

And there is another function for that elaborate beak; it would have been a formidable weapon! During the mating season the sound of the crashing of beaks would have reverberated across the island as male suitors squared up to each other.

These fights would have been fierce with that huge beak pulling chunks of downy feathers out of the rump of the overthrown male. The reward made the battle worthwhile however, with the victorious male securing his mate for life.

Giant Moa

Dinornis robustus

THE DISCOVERY

It was in 1839, when Richard Owen was 35, that a man dropped in on him at the Royal College of Surgeons in London and presented him with a piece of bone. Owen was fast becoming known as one of the greatest anatomists of the Victorian era and John Rule had travelled over 11,000 miles from New Zealand, an archipelago on the other side of the world, to see him. Rule claimed that the bone wrapped in tatty brown paper belonged to a huge, extinct, monstrous bird called a moa. With a sideways glance Owen quickly dismissed him, saying that the bone was clearly a fragment from the leg of a large land animal. At about six inches long the fragment of bone had thick walls and sturdy proportions and Owen believed this was in keeping with a four-legged animal like a cow. Showing admirable perseverance, John Rule persuaded Owen to take a closer look and sure enough, upon further inspection, there was a feature of the bone that caught Owen's eye.

First piece of moa bone, found between 1831 and 1836, showing its honeycomb structure.

Richard Owen and the skeleton of Dinornis maximus, c. 1877.

The internal structure of the bone was composed of a honeycomb lattice rather than being a hollow cavity once filled with marrow. Owen painstakingly compared the piece of bone with the bones of 14 other species, including those of humans, kangaroos and even a giant tortoise. He realised that the latticed, porous internal bone structure he saw before him was something unique to the skeletons of birds.

John Rule was right – a giant bird had once roamed across New Zealand! Owen deduced that the bird, larger than any known, would have been too heavy to fly, so a search began in earnest for the remains of a giant flightless bird, the moa.

Owen requested that any New Zealander in possession of moa bones send them his way. The world was amazed when, four years later, the first full skeleton was exhibited in London, made up of the disarticulated bones of several giant moas. Owen reconstructed it rather like an ostrich, and it really was a monster at three metres in height.

A competition ensued as to who could find the tallest skeleton, with some unscrupulous Victorian collectors even inserting additional vertebrae to claim the prize!

HOW DOES A FLIGHTLESS BIRD
FIND ITS WAY ONTO AN ISLAND?

Unlike other flightless birds the moa has absolutely no remnant of wings, not even stumps like those of the dodo or kiwi. So how did a flightless bird like the moa reach New Zealand, an archipelago some 1,200 miles east of Australia in the South Pacific Ocean? Well, the continents of our planet are constantly changing as a result of plate tectonics. New landmasses are being created as undersea volcanoes spurt molten rock from deep within our planet, and old landmasses

sink beneath the Earth's crust. All the while, the tectonic plates on which our continents sit are moving at a rate of about three centimetres a year, roughly the same rate at which our fingernails grow.

So, around 200 million years ago the world was a very different place, with the southern hemisphere dominated by a super-continent known as Gondwana.

The moa's native habitat,
New Zealand

 GIANT MOA

Gondwana extended the whole way from the South Pole to the equator at a time when the Earth's climate was much warmer than it is today. Gondwana was then host to a huge variety of flora and fauna that thrived for many millions of years. However, about 180 million years ago Gondwana began to break up and, roughly 100 million years later, New Zealand broke away and drifted north and east. Some of the animals and plants of Gondwana became trapped and isolated by the South Pacific Ocean on the landmass that became the islands of New Zealand.

Some of these animals were the ancestors of moa. They may have once been able to fly, but over many millions of years living on an island with abundant food and no ground-dwelling predators, they lost that ability and grew larger, with some species becoming giants.

Giant moa model in the Natural History Museum, London, commissioned by Lord Rothschild c. 1900

WHAT DID THE MOA LOOK LIKE?

After the rush to find moa bones, skeletons were quickly assembled in museums across the world. In around 1900, Lord Rothschild commissioned a reconstruction of a giant moa which still stands in Central Hall in the Natural History Museum, London. Its feathers are from an emu, likely to have been sourced from zoos or other specimens arriving at the taxidermist's workshop.

In the museum there is also a skeleton of one of the largest moa species, the South Island *Dinornis robustus*, pieced together by Richard Owen. It stands upright rather like an ostrich does today. But if we were to bring this moa to life we would discover that in fact it would have looked quite different!

○ *Watercolour of a giant moa by Frederick William Frohawk from Extinct Birds (1907) by Lord Rothschild.*

Did You Know?

Moa were actually very long birds, rather than tall birds as the early depictions would have them. The moa head was held only slightly above the level of the back.

A myth prevailed until the 1980s that the giant moas were grassland grazing birds. However, giant moa skeletons have been found with the contents of their gizzards preserved, alongside gastroliths, pebble-sized stones which the giant moa needed to help grind up its tough, fibrous diet. Their specially adapted beaks confirm their preference for snipping twigs off low trees and shrubs, indicating that giant moas lived mostly in the forests of New Zealand.

A few mummified remains also have preserved feathers so we can really guess at what the giant moa might have looked like. Their narrow, ribbon-like feathers were reddish-brown, very different to the strong, stiff and asymmetric feathers found on the wings of birds that fly.

We know from the structure of the neck and skull that the giant moa would have held its head stooped like emus and cassowaries do today, with its head only slightly above the level of its back and its neck attached behind its skull rather than beneath. If the giant moa lived in a forested habitat this would have been to its advantage. An upright stance allows an ostrich to scan the horizon for predators in its African habitat, but in the forest a long neck would be a hindrance for a giant moa as it tried to navigate through the dense vegetation.

◗ *Mummified moa head, found in a central Otago cave in New Zealand.*

DID THE MOA HAVE A PREDATOR?

Recent research has revealed that what were thought to be the remains of several species of moa of different sizes in fact belonged to just one species. The female, *Dinornis robustus*, was up to 150% taller and 280% heavier than the males. She could weigh around 200 kilograms, as much as three grown men, and if she were to crane up her neck she could certainly have reached three metres, making her one of the tallest birds in the world.

Unbelievably, even a bird of this size had a predator in the forests of New Zealand. With talons the size of a tiger's claw and a beak as large as a kitchen knife, *Harpagornis* was the largest eagle that has ever existed. The largest would have weighed up to 15 kilograms, which is about as close as can be to the theoretical limit at which a bird can fly.

Originally *Harpagornis* was thought to be a scavenger of dead or dying giant moas; but in 1991 scientists realised that terrible wounds in giant moa hip bones exactly matched the enormous grasp of *Harpagornis's* talons. Like other forest eagles, they were ambush predators, waiting patiently on a low branch for their prey to appear below. With a wingspan of up to three metres it could swoop, folding its wings to manoeuvre through the trees, before swinging its feet forward and striking the unsuspecting moa with incredible force. It would sink one of its 10-centimetre claws into the pelvis of the moa and the other just at the base of the neck, piercing through the

feathers and flesh, crushing the moa's internal organs and rupturing its major blood vessels. Some moa skeletons reveal that the eagle would strike repeatedly with its talons and hold on whilst driving the talons of its other foot into the blood vessels at the base of the moa's neck and even into the skull. Once the moa was dead the *Harpagornis* would tear into the carcass with its enormous beak, just like a vulture dealing with a dead zebra on the African plains.

The New Zealand Warriors from
A journal of a voyage to the South Seas
1773 by Sydney Parkinson.

 GIANT MOA

HOW DID THE MOA BECOME EXTINCT?

So was it predation by *Harpagornis* that led to the extinction of the giant moa? In fact, the normal prey of a *Harpagornis* were the large flightless rails and waterfowl found in abundance in the forests of the eastern South Island of New Zealand. And there were no eagles outside the eastern South Island. So how did the giant moa become extinct?

By the time Owen had described the moa and revealed it to the world it had been extinct for over 400 years. There was, however, one group of early settlers in New Zealand who came face to face with the moa: the Maori. Ancestors of the Maori arrived on canoes from the Pacific Islands and colonised New Zealand just after 1300 AD. They quickly established communities along the coasts of both islands.

The Maori had a strong tradition of hunting and were fierce warriors who used psychology and intimidation in warfare – the haka (war dance) was intended to give their rivals a preview of things to come. Their main source of meat came from seals, moa and fish. Once they had consumed the moa for food they would utilise its bones to make ornaments, fishhooks and bird spear-points, and even collected and incubated moa eggs until an embryo developed. Within 100 or so years of their arrival in New Zealand all the species of moa, six species of flightless rail, many waterfowl and indeed 40% of all the bird fauna had become extinct. The demise of *Harpagornis* soon followed.

SCAN HERE

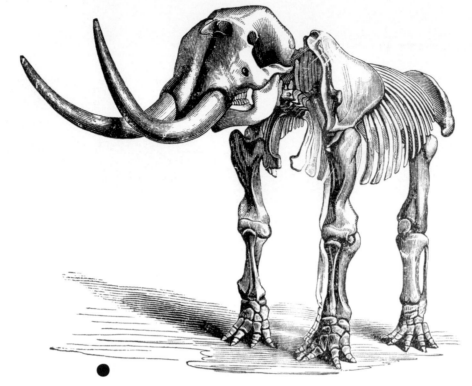

Profile

Period:
They had become extinct
13,000 years ago

Habitat:
Woodlands and forests
of North America

Size:
HEIGHT
Male: 2.34 m (7.7 ft) -
2.8 m (9 ft 2 in) at the shoulder
WEIGHT
Up to 5.5 tonnes

Diet:
Coniferous twigs and low
lying vegetation

American Mastodon

Mammut americanum

THE DISCOVERY

In the summer of 1705 a Dutch tenant farmer discovered a tooth the size of a man's fist as he worked his land in the Hudson River Valley, New York State. The tooth was traded for a glass of rum to a local politician who eagerly made a gift of his prize to Lord Cornbury, the outlandish governor of New York. Cornbury labelled it the "tooth of a giant" and soon the "monstrous creature" it belonged to was celebrated across the globe, known only as the "incognitum", the unknown species.

PEALE'S "MAMMOTH"

A portrait artist, Charles Wilson Peale, first examined the incognitum bones in 1783, an experience which was to set him on a lifelong mission to discover the mysteries of the natural world. He ventured to the Hudson River Valley where a farmer, John Masten, had found the remains of "an animal of uncommon magnitude". Excavation began in 1801 and soon Peale had amassed enough bones to build a near complete skeleton.

Peale exaggerated the height of the skeleton so that it stood well over three metres at the shoulder and he positioned the tusks downward as if it was a voracious predator. This was one of the first and largest fossil skeletons to be built and, unsurprisingly, it astonished the nation. It became known as Peale's mammoth.

Mastodon tusk unearthed at Ludlow, Kentucky, six feet ten inches long, weighing 156 pounds and 9 ounces.

◔ *Illustration of Peale's mammoth*

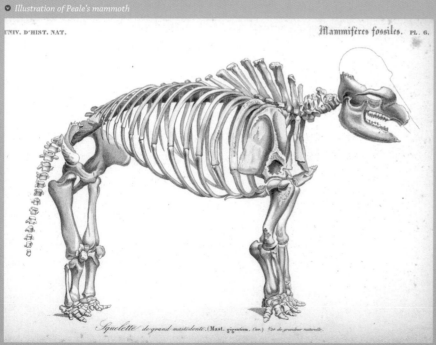

◔ Exhumation of the Mastodon *by Peale, 1806*
Credit: Science Photo Library

◎ Poster for Koch's Missouri Leviathan exhibition
at the Egyptian Hall, Piccadilly, 1842.
Credit: Alexander Turnbull Library, New Zealand

At about the same time there were reports of large bones and tusks being unearthed in the vicinity of Kimmswick, Missouri. In 1839 Dr Albert Koch, a German immigrant who was the owner of the St. Louis Museum, investigated these reports and began an excavation along the banks of Rock Creek, Missouri. He was so amazed by the size of the bones he found that he thought he had discovered a new animal and he named his find the Missouri Leviathan.

An entrepreneur and showman, Koch grossly exaggerated the size of his Missouri Leviathan by adding in extra bones and even blocks of wood to make the skeleton appear larger. When it went on display in Pittsburgh on 19th August 1841, he charged 50 cents a ticket and declared it stood "32 feet long and 15 feet in height; the breast is 10 feet broad; the extreme length of its enormous tusks is 21 feet from point to point."

The following year Koch travelled to Europe and exhibited the Missouri Leviathan in the Egyptian Hall, in London's fashionable Piccadilly, charging a shilling for entry.

His poster stated that, "The Missouri Leviathan, between whose legs the Mammoth, and even the mighty Iguanodon may easily have crept, is universally acknowledged by men of science to be the greatest phenomenon ever discovered in Natural History".

Richard Owen, a rising star at the British Museum in the field of comparative anatomy and, later, the driving force behind the creation of the Natural History Museum, was intrigued and paid his shilling for the chance to observe the mighty Missouri Leviathan. He immediately recognised its grossly fabricated pose and was quick to declare this at a meeting of the Geological Society of London.

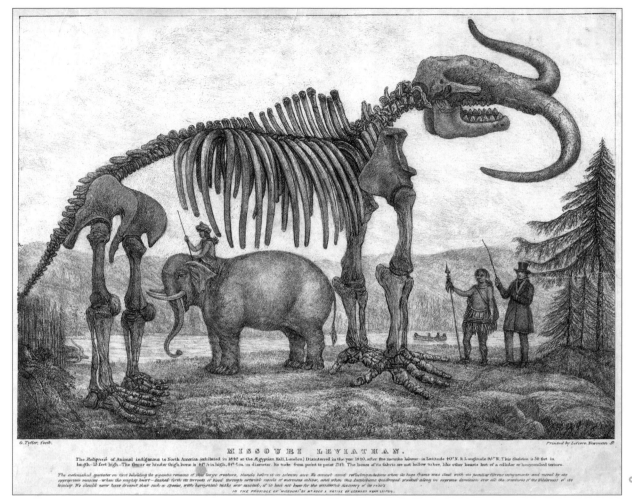

MISSOURI LEVIATHAN.

The *Reliquiæ* of Animal indigenous to North America (exhibited in 1842 at the Ægyptian Hall, London) Disinterred in the year 1840, after five months labour in Latitude 40°N. & Longitude 95°W. This Skeleton is 30 feet in length—15 feet high.—The femur or hinder thigh bone is 4ft 6in high, 8ft 6in in diameter. Its tusks from point to point 21ft. The bones of its fabric are not hollow tubes, like other beasts but of a cellular or honeycombed texture.

The astonished spectator on first beholding the gigantic remains of this large creature, stands before it in solemn awe He cannot avoid reflecting whence when its huge frame was clad with its familiar fibrous integuments and moved by its appropriate muscles when the mighty heart dashed forth its torrents of blood through arterial vessels of enormous calibre, and when this lumphious Quadruped walked along in supreme dominion over all the creatures of the Wilderness of his lonicity. We should never have dreamt that such a species, with horizontal tusks now assailed, if it had not been for the wonderful discovery of its relics.

IN THE PROVINCE OF "MISSOURI" BY M.* KOCH A NATIVE OF GERMANY NEAR LEIPSIC.

◀ *Illustration of Koch's Missouri Leviathan.*

He even reworked the skeleton, producing a huge, seven-foot-long drawing of it in its correct position. However, the British public were so taken with the Missouri Leviathan that the exhibition stayed open for a whole year before travelling on to Dublin and then Germany. It was not until 1844 that the shrewd Albert Koch stopped over in London on his way back to America, to complete an important transaction. Despite recognising Koch's magnified reconstruction, Owen had also noticed that when corrected, the Missouri Leviathan would be a particularly fine specimen and so he persuaded the British Museum to purchase it. Koch received a down payment of US$2,000 and a further US$1,000 a year for the rest of his life, which in the end amounted to US$23,000!

As soon as Owen got his hands on the Missouri Leviathan he brought it back to the museum for closer inspection.

He removed the excess bones and wooden blocks and twisted the tusks around so they were positioned correctly. It still stands in the Natural History Museum today at a corrected height of three metres.

Mammut americanum, the
American mastodon lived only
in North America. They never
spread to South America,
perhaps because their preferred
food source did not extend that
far south; they may have been
specialised to eat only a few
varieties of plant.

⊙ *Tooth of an American mastodon
(Mammut americanum)*

So what type of creature was the Missouri Leviathan, the *incognitum* and Peale's mammoth?

There were all in fact American mastodons, *Mammut americanum*, a relative of the mammoth and the African and Asian elephants we know today. It was that giant, five-pound tooth which gave the American mastodon its name. To the young French anatomist Georges Cuvier, the conical cusps looked like breasts. So in 1806, he named the incognitum "mastodon," from the Greek mastos (for "breast") and odont (for "tooth").

WHAT DID THE AMERICAN MASTODON EAT?

When compared to those of a mammoth or elephant, the giant tooth of an American mastodon appears to be quite different. The conical cusps, which gave the American mastodon its name, reveal that it was a herbivore like its cousins. Unlike mammoths, however, whose flat, ridged molars were used for grazing on grasses, mastodons' teeth were used for clipping and crushing twigs, leaves and other parts of shrubs and trees. At any one time, the American mastodon had two or three molars on each side of its jaw which were vital for allowing it to consume huge quantities of vegetation every day. To sustain its appetite over its lifetime, worn molars would fall out at the front of the jaw, and new molars would form in the back and move forward to replace the worn teeth.

WHAT DID THE AMERICAN MASTODON LOOK LIKE?

Unlike modern elephants, American mastodons were covered with a thick coat of shaggy hair. This was vital for keeping them warm as temperatures in North America during the Pleistocene epoch could dip to well below freezing.

The tusks of the American mastodon were long and curved and though both male and female mastodons possessed such tusks, those of the male were considerably larger, typically reaching as long as two and a half metres. It seems likely that they would have used their tusks to deter and fight off predators, or to tussle with other mastodons over food or space.

Two fighting African elephants,
Loxodonta africana.

FIERCE BATTLES

The tusks of male mastodons were larger than the female which suggests they also used them as weapons against other males as they fought for the right to mate with available females, much like elephants do today. Male bull elephants are known to fight in seasonal, hormonally-charged battles to show their dominance and win desired mates. Scars discovered on mastodon tusks suggest that, rather than being passive creatures, they too fought in fierce battles each year during the breeding season. The American mastodons might have utilised their long, upward-curving tusks to deliver an up-thrusting blow, piercing through the neck or skull of their rival.

 AMERICAN MASTODON

SOCIALITY

In the same way that the rings of a tree reveal its age, the tusks of a mastodon grew constantly throughout its life, documenting a precise record of its growth and health. American mastodons grew slowly, taking a relatively long time to reach maturity, indicating that they would have relied on parental care, such as that provided in modern elephant herds.

Perhaps adult male mastodons only gathered together for duels during the breeding season, whereas the females and their young lived in small family groups until they reached maturity.

◔ *Front view of a skull of a Mastodon, Zygolophodon atticus, - did fossils like these give rise to the myth of the Cyclops?*

◔ *Illustration of an American mastodon,* Mammut americanum.

MYTH OF THE CYCLOPS

Fossils of a primitive mastodon, *Zygolophodon atticus*, which lived throughout the Miocene, 23 to 5 million years ago, have been found across Greece. Paleontologists today recognise that the pronounced hole in the centre of its skull suggests it once had a large trunk, like its cousins the elephants and other species of mastodon. However, for the ancient Greeks, who regularly dug up its fossil skeletons, these skulls may have fuelled the myth of the fearsome one-eyed Cyclops!

 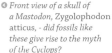

HOW DID THE MASTODON BECOME EXTINCT?

We know that the mastodon in North America became extinct around 13,000 years ago, at the end of the Pleistocene era. Why? The reason for this mass extinction is a matter of much debate and still remains something of a mystery. A controversial theory proposed in the 1960s claimed that the evolution and global expansion of humans, *Homo sapiens*, by the end of the Pleistocene was the cause. But would early humans have been sufficiently numerous and had technology advanced enough to wipe out whole species? Another theory blames a shift in the global climate as their extinction roughly coincides with the global warming at the end of the last ice age.

The answer is still up for debate but many scientists agree that a combination of climate change and hunting may have been the cause for such a significant global extinction event.

SCAN HERE

 AMERICAN MASTODON

Giant Ground Sloth

Glossotherium robustum

THE DISCOVERY

Along with the American mastodon, the giant ground sloth was one of the first animals to be recognised as extinct. Before their discovery it would have been sacrilege even to suggest that one of "God's creatures" could become extinct as all fossils found were thought to have belonged to creatures still alive somewhere on the planet.

It was in 1796 that the famous French comparative anatomist Baron Georges Cuvier received some drawings from Madrid. They were of a skeleton which had been brought to Madrid from the Spanish colonies in South America nine years earlier. At six metres in length from head to tail, the skeleton clearly belonged to a giant, and George Cuvier named it *Megatherium americanum*, which translates as "Great Beast from America". Cuvier recognised characteristics in the fossil's bones and teeth that were

 GIANT GROUND SLOTH

shared with a group of living animals – the tree sloths, anteaters and armadillos. He also realised that an animal of this size would surely have been spotted if it were still alive, so he proposed that the fossil must belong to an extinct creature.

After this initial discovery, the remains of other giant sloths were uncovered and avidly sought after by museums all over the world.

More than 30 years later, in 1831, the young naturalist Charles Darwin embarked on an epic voyage on the H.M.S *Beagle*. Darwin was to be companion to the ship's Captain, Robert Fitzroy, as the *Beagle* mapped in detail the coastline of South America. The voyage was supposed to take two years but instead took nearer five, and Darwin found himself surveying and exploring the continent of South America for much of that time. An avid naturalist, he filled endless notebooks with thoughts, sketches and observations and collected thousands of specimens which he carefully packaged up in crates and shipped back to the United Kingdom.

Darwin was to describe this voyage as, "by far the most important event in my life", and his experiences in South America were to form the foundation of his theory of evolution, expounded in his book *On the Origin of Species*.

When Darwin returned home to the United Kingdom with a treasure trove of fossils, he was introduced by his friend Charles Lyell to Richard Owen, the driving force behind the creation of the Natural History Museum. Recognising Owen as one of the greatest comparative anatomists of the time, Darwin gave him the task of identifying his fossil bones from South America. Darwin had unearthed the remains of nine great mammals in one location in Patagonia and he had referred most of them to the giant ground sloth *Megatherium americanum*, partly because it was the only

◗ *Reconstructed skeleton of Megatherium americanum, a giant ground sloth at the Natural History Museum, London.*

large mammal known at the time. Upon closer inspection Richard Owen reclassified these mammals and, in the process, described for the world another ground sloth species which he named *Mylodon darwinii*, the first of many species to be named after Darwin.

Like Cuvier before him, Darwin was struck by the similarities between these giant skeletons and those of modern tree sloths. He began to consider the connectedness of all species, extant and extinct, another step in the formulation of his theory of evolution.

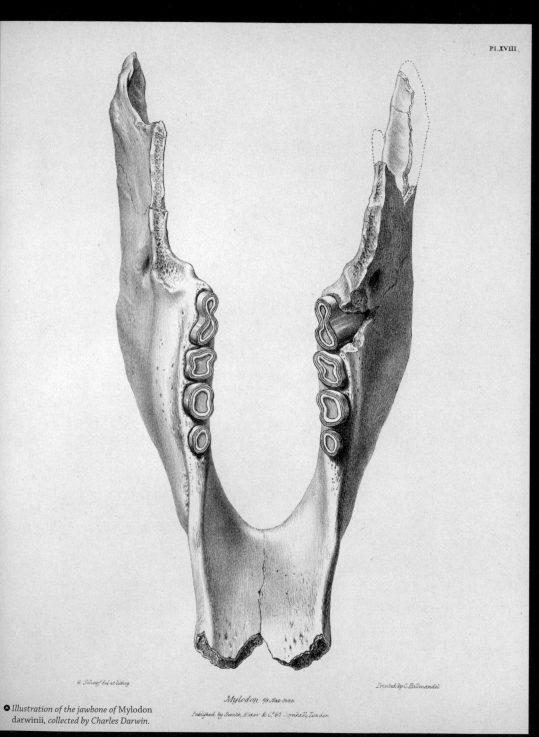

PL.XVIII.

G. Scharf del et lithog

Printed by C. Hullmandel

Mylodon. 2/3 Nat Size.

Published by Smith, Elder & Co. 65 Cornhill, London.

 Illustration of the jawbone of Mylodon darwinii, *collected by Charles Darwin.*

RIDING HIS HOBBY.

 Cartoon of Richard Owen from Cartoon portraits and biographical sketches of men of the day, 1873, *by Frederick Waddy.*

THE FEUD

Owen and Darwin, two rising stars of the Victorian scientific community, were quick to forge a friendship. However, they also had profound scientific disagreements, and these, coupled with Owen's bitter jealousy of Darwin's success and Darwin's suspicions of Owen's attempts to discredit him, would cripple their friendship entirely.

When *On the Origin of Species* was published in 1859 it was met with disdain by many in the largely Anglican scientific community of the day. None were more opposed than Richard Owen, believing in the early part of his career that each species had been uniquely designed and created by God, perfectly adapted for its lifestyle.

This difference of opinion is even reflected in the design of the Natural History Museum itself. At a time when Darwin was proposing a link between all extinct and living species, Owen was determined that the terracotta sculptures of living and extinct species adorning the building should be kept separate – with extinct animals decorating the east wing and living decorating the west. Their feud reached its head when Owen wrote an anonymous review of *On the Origin of Species* in the *Edinburgh Review*, criticising Darwin's reasoning and that of his followers. This rivalry captured the public's imagination and was celebrated in poetry, play and even in cartoon form.

This caricature of Owen (see opposite page) was printed in *Vanity Fair* and perhaps best sums up how Owen was perceived by some of his peers towards the end of his career. It describes him as a wicked and simple-minded creature. Was Owen as wicked as reports stated? We know he was far from simple-minded but certainly there was no love lost between Owen and Darwin. As Darwin famously commented, "I used to be ashamed of hating him so much, but now I will carefully cherish my hatred and contempt to the last days of my life".

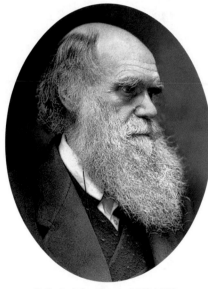
● *Charles Robert Darwin (1809-1882)*

● *Sir Richard Owen (1804-1892)*

COULD GIANT GROUND SLOTHS STILL EXIST?

After Cuvier's description of the giant ground sloth *Megatherium americanum* and Darwin's discovery of the bones of *Mylodon darwinii*, expeditions were launched to unearth more remains across South America. In 1895, a German landowner, Captain Hermann Eberhardt, stumbled across a shaggy, reddish hide in an enormous cave on his land in Chile.

The strange, furry piece of hide was hung up on a tree at the mouth of the cave and became a curiosity for passers-by. The fur appeared to be so fresh that it was presumed to belong to a living animal, but which one? A year later, a team of Swedish explorers passed by the cave on their way to Tierra del Fuego. They were intrigued by the piece of hide still hanging on the tree,

Glossotherium robustum's native habitat, **South America**

Giant ground sloths were a diverse group of large, hairy sloths with massive jaws, blunt snouts, and powerful clawed limbs. They lived 23 million years ago to 10,000 years ago in North and South America.

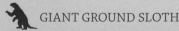 GIANT GROUND SLOTH

The fossilised skin and dung of the extinct giant ground sloth, Mylodon darwinii, *found in South America.*

and in particular by the bony, pebble-shaped discs that lined the underside of the skin. They cut off a section and sent it back to Europe to be studied in more detail. It was not long before word of this mysterious 'cowhide' spread, and a prominent scientist, Dr Francisco Moreno, ventured to the cave to investigate. He deduced that the hide must have belonged to the giant ground sloth *Mylodon* due to the bony discs that were exclusively found on this group of South American mammals. Could the giant ground sloth, *Mylodon*, have still existed in South America? Several years later, the Swedish team returned and excavated inside the cave. They unearthed further skeletal remains, all buried beneath

Dr Francisco Moreno (1852 - 1919)

a layer of well-preserved ground sloth dung. Like the skin, this dung appeared so fresh that the Swedish explorers were sure it must have been recently deposited by a living creature. Over the course of the next century numerous expeditions were launched and many unsubstantiated sightings of giant ground sloths were reported. We now know, with modern carbon-dating techniques, that the remains discovered in that cave were between 12,000 and 16,000 years old. So how did they look so fresh? Dr Moreno was the first to point out that the conditions in that cold, dark cave in Chile were ideal for freeze-drying, perfectly preserving the fur and dung for thousands of years.

◆ *Artist's impression of a Pleistocene landscape in Patagonia.*

HOW DID THE GIANT GROUND SLOTHS BECOME EXTINCT?

There were many different species of giant ground sloth and they were once so numerous that they roamed from the tip of Patagonia all the way to Alaska. They thrived during a period called the Pleistocene between 2.6 million and 11,700 years ago. This was the time of the giant mammals, or the megafauna.

South America would have looked very different to what we see now. Alongside these giant sloths were strange-looking animals such as the armoured glyptodons – relatives of armadillos but the size of a modern hippo – macrauchenids, rhino-like toxodons, bears and sabre-toothed cats.

The last giant ground sloths seem to have died out by about 10,000 years ago, soon after the human colonisation of the Americas. They became extinct along with the other megafauna from North and South America. Scientists have for years been debating whether hunting by humans alone could be the cause for such a series of extinctions. Other theories suggested for their extinction are climate change and disease, or perhaps their demise was a result of a combination of these factors.

 GIANT GROUND SLOTH

MEGATHERIUM SKELETON IN THE MUSEUM

Megatherium was the largest of the ground sloth species, reaching a height of six metres! The Natural History Museum (then part of the British Museum) purchased *Megatherium* material, collected near Buenos Aires, from a Señor de Angelis in 1845. Plaster casts of these bones were made and added to bones from a further collection of *Megatherium* remains at the Royal College of Surgeons. A few missing bones, mainly ribs and vertebrae, were modelled and

inserted, and in 1849 a cast of a composite skeleton of *Megatherium americanum* was revealed.

Originally the skeleton was mounted standing on all four limbs, like the original Madrid specimen described by Cuvier. We now know that *Megatherium* often supported its weight on its back legs, and so the skeleton was re-mounted to reflect this change in our understanding.

GLOSSOTHERIUM ROBUSTUM IN THE MUSEUM

At three metres in length, *Glossotherium robustum* is smaller than its giant cousin, the *Megatherium*. It was discovered in alluvial deposits near Buenos Aires in Argentina and was purchased by the museum in 1885. We know it was a vegetarian so what did it use those enormous claws for?

GIANT GROUND SLOTHS IN LIFE

The ground sloths existed relatively recently in our planet's history, becoming extinct some 10,000 years ago. Since the first fossil bones were discovered, scientists have been piecing together the clues to gain a better understanding of what they might have looked like and how they might have behaved. Preserved hides, such as the ones found in the Cueva del Milodon, have given us an impression of what these giant beasts might have looked like, with the bony discs under their fur presumably acting like a chainmail, protecting them against predators.

Fossilised footprints have been found in South America, revealing that the ground sloths walked in a peculiar way, on the outside of their feet and with all their toes off the ground. By analysing their skeletons and fossilised tracks, scientists have also shown that some sloths were bipedal – capable of walking on two legs.

If the ground sloths were bipedal, then it would have freed up their arms for other tasks. We know from their dung that giant sloths were probably vegetarians, so surely those huge claws would have been useful for digging up tubers and roots and selecting the finest leaves.

> The smaller ground sloths, such as *Glossotherium robustum*, also had formidable claws.

Scientists have suggested that the huge arms and claws of *Megatherium* weren't used for digging, but instead were capable of fast and even aggressive actions. The mechanics of its biceps might have made it possible for the animal to have lifted and carried heavy weights – for example, turning armoured prey such as the *Glyptodon* upside down to expose its softer parts – and for caching large food pieces in a safer place. If the *Megatherium* was in fact a carnivore, it would have been the largest mammalian hunter to have ever existed!

The smaller ground sloths such as *Glossotherium robustum* also had formidable claws. However, scientists have speculated that their smaller body size, coupled with powerful claws and forearms, might have made them expert diggers. And not just digging for food! Enormous burrows, one metre in diameter and as long as 40 metres, have been discovered, exposed along sea cliffs in Argentina. Grooves on the walls of these palaeoburrows, 30 centimetres long and four centimetres in width, exactly match the size and shape of the ground sloth's well-developed claws. Why would such a large sloth dig a burrow? Well, believe it or not, these giant sloths did have a predator: the sabre-toothed cat, *Smilodon*.

SCAN HERE

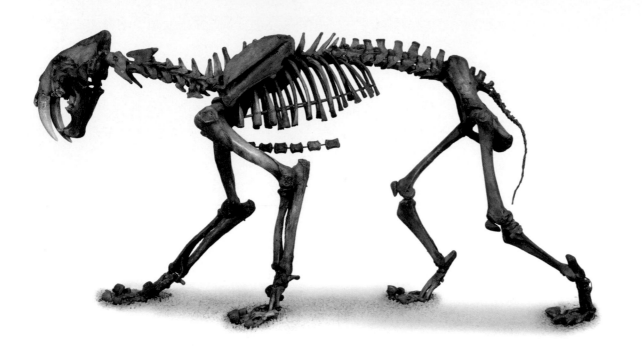

Profile

Period:
They had become extinct 13,000 years ago

Habitat:
North America

Size:
HEIGHT
1 metre at the shoulder
WEIGHT
160-280 kg (353 - 617 lb)
LENGTH
175 cm (5.7 ft.) rump to snout

Diet:
Bison, camels, prehistoric horses, ground sloths and mastodons.

Sabre-Toothed Cat

Smilodon fatalis

THE DISCOVERY

⊙ *Natural gas bubble slowly escaping from the Tar Pits at La Brea.*

In the heart of central Los Angeles, just south of Sunset Boulevard, there is a surprising site that you might be excused for thinking was a Hollywood film set.

Many thousands of years ago, a sticky black crude oil or asphalt began to ooze out of the Earth's crust, engulfing this small pocket of land and, with it, any unsuspecting passers-by. Each bubbling pit is a window into our planet's past, perfectly preserving any animals that were unfortunate enough to stray too near.

As a result, the La Brea tar pits, at just 23 acres in size, are one of the richest fossil reserves in the world, yielding over three million specimens in the last century and, still to this day, they are an active

 SABRE-TOOTHED CAT

palaeontological site. Over 600 species of plants and animals have been unearthed, including the fossilised remains of sabre-toothed cats, dire wolves, mastodons, mammoths and giant ground sloths.

The discovery of marine shells at the site suggests that Native Americans used them to transport the asphalt, which acted as a glue to waterproof their baskets and as a caulk to seal their canoes. The first written reference to the tar pits was in 1769, in the diary of a Franciscan friar, Juan Crespi. Recording the expedition of some Spanish explorers, he wrote, "While crossing the basin the scouts reported having seen some geysers of tar issuing from the ground like springs; it boils up molten, and the water runs to one side and the tar to the other. We christened them Los Volcanes de Brea (the Tar Volcanoes)." The early settlers in Los Angeles used the asphalt as fuel and as waterproofing for their roofs. When they uncovered bones they presumed they were the remains of domestic animals.

⊙ *William Denton*

⊙ *The skull of a sabre-toothed cat, discovered at La Brea tar pits, LA.*

It was many years later that the scientific significance of the tar pits was recognised. In 1875, an Englishman called William Denton was invited to visit the Hancock family, who owned the land on which the tar pits were found. He was given a canine tooth, and so large was this tooth that he instantly recognised that it belonged to nothing alive on the planet at that time, but was rather the canine of a sabre-toothed cat. Denton published his find in the journal of the Boston Society of Natural History but, to his dismay, the scientific community paid little interest.

It wasn't until the start of the twentieth century that the Hancock family stopped mining the asphalt commercially and started to explore the large oil deposits found on their land. A geologist called William Orcutt was sent to investigate and was amazed to find the bones of many extinct species in the asphalt seeps. Excavations began in earnest and, by 1915, millions of bones had been removed from La Brea by amateurs and institutions alike. Hancock recognised the scientific value of his land and entrusted the site to the Los Angeles Natural History Museum to prevent more fossils being removed.

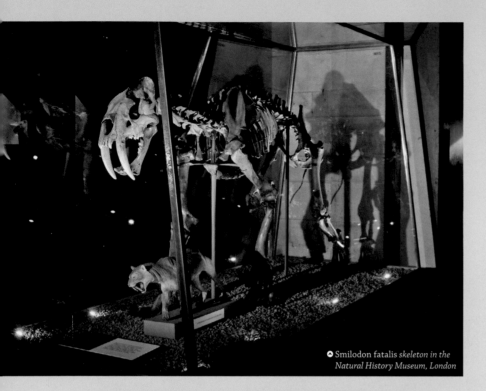
Smilodon fatalis *skeleton in the Natural History Museum, London*

SABRE-TOOTHED CAT IN THE MUSEUM

The bones of the sabre-toothed cat, *Smilodon fatalis*, are the second most common remains found in the La Brea tar pits. In total, the remains of some 2,000 *Smilodon fatalis* have been found there.

Something apparent to many visitors to the Natural History Museum, London is how exceptionally well preserved the skeleton of the sabre-toothed cat is. Its condition is in fact a result of the place where it died. As the unsuspecting cat became trapped in the gooey asphalt it quickly perished, succumbing to dehydration and famine. The asphalt into which it sank seeped into every bone, turning them a dark-brown colour. The lighter petroleum evaporated from the asphalt, leaving behind a solid substance which encased the bones, preserving them perfectly.

Location of La Brea tar pits, **Los Angeles, North America**

Sabre-toothed cats probably preyed on juvenile animals – giant ground sloths, prehistoric horses and mastodons. They weren't averse to a bit of scavenging either - we know because sabre-toothed cats that feasted on dead or dying animals caught in the La Brea tar pits outside Los Angeles often became stuck themselves - 2,000 of them in this location alone.

Extinct mammals at the La Brea tar pits, Los Angeles, California.

Smilodon would have caught its prey in an ambush attack, held it still, and used those massive teeth to inflict puncture wounds until its unfortunate victim bled to death.

Mass of bones of prehistoric animals found in asphalt deposits in La Brea, Los Angeles.

WINDOW INTO THE PAST

Apart from the impressive fossils of large mammals, La Brea tar pits have also preserved insects, molluscs, seeds, dust, leaves and even pollen grains. What can such a treasure trove of fossils reveal?

During the Pleistocene epoch from 40,000 years ago, the area that is now downtown Los Angeles would have been cooler and moister. Much of the vegetation preserved in La Brea is similar to the vegetation that would still have existed in Los Angeles today had the sprawling city not got in the way, yet most of the larger animals found in La Brea are no longer found in North America – the long-horned bison, mastodons, mammoths, native horses, camels and sabre-toothed cats.

In traditional ecosystems to this day, herbivores usually outnumber carnivores – just think of the plains of East Africa. Strangely, however, 90 per cent of the skeletal remains found in La Brea belong to carnivores – the sabre-toothed cats, dire wolves and lions. Was the Pleistocene a period ruled by voracious carnivores? In fact, carnivores were no more common than in modern ecosystems like East Africa. Scientists believe that carnivores were attracted in their numbers to La Brea by the distress sounds of the trapped grazing animals. As they approached to take advantage of an easy meal, they too became victims of the sticky trap of tar.

FEARSOME FANGS

We know that *Smilodon fatalis* was a fearsome predator that did not have to rely on scavenging to get a meal. With a body weight of up to 280 kilograms, it was considerably heavier than a lion today and most likely would have preyed on the juveniles of giant sloths and mastodons, and adults of smaller (but still quite large) mammals such as prehistoric horses. Its considerable weight, coupled with canines that could grow to 17 centimetres, would have made *Smilodon fatalis* a formidable hunter. It had a huge bite and could open its jaws to an angle approaching 130 degrees, which is about twice that of a modern lion – with fangs that long it needed an enormous gape to get food in its mouth! But how did it use its fangs?

Well, if we bring this skeleton to life we might get a better idea of how it hunted. Scientists have analysed their canines and discovered that they were surprisingly brittle, with a bite only one-third as powerful as that of modern lions. Also, unlike cheetahs and lions, their skeletons show that they had a bobtail rather than a long tail to help with balance. So, rather than risking damaging their canines by chasing their prey over long distances before wrestling them to the ground and delivering a fatal bite to the neck, we now think that sabre-toothed cats were ambush predators. They would have stalked their prey before pouncing and using their huge bulk to hold them down. With one claw on the cheek and one on the shoulder they could immobilise their unfortunate victim before biting down on the soft flesh of the neck, piercing the jugular and severing the main arteries. The animal had to remain still or the *Smilodon* risked hitting bone and fracturing its brittle teeth. Once the deed was done, the *Smilodon* would wait for its prey to bleed to death before tucking in.

○ *Fossilised skull of a Sabre-toothed cat.*

 SABRE-TOOTHED CAT

Did You Know?

They had a huge bite and could open their jaws 128 degrees - twice as wide as a modern lion. They had to, in order to get their massive fangs around their prey!

HUNTING IN PACKS

Skeletons discovered at La Brea include bones that show evidence of serious injuries in life, as well as degenerative diseases such as arthritis. And some of these bones show signs of healing. How could a *Smilodon* survive these injuries, let alone begin to heal? Well, it seems likely that the *Smilodon* lived in packs rather like a pride of lions today. Rather than leaving an injured cat to die, members of the pack would have cared for it and allowed it to share in their kill.

● *Illustration of a Clovis hunter*
Credit: Courtesy of Joe Venus

WHY DID THE *SMILODON* BECOME EXTINCT?

Along with the American mastodon, *Smilodon fatalis* became extinct in North America about 13,000 years ago. These were not two isolated events. In fact, between 13,500 years ago and 11,500 years ago, 72 per cent of the megafauna of North America became extinct, which is actually quite sudden if you consider our planet's four-and-a-half-billion-year history. What caused this major extinction? At about this time the global climate was changing and our planet was entering a warm spell following the last ice age. At the same time, the first humans, the Clovis people, migrated into North America. Could these Palaeo-Indians have been responsible for hunting the megafauna of North America to extinction? More likely is that the megafauna was already in a fragile state following the global climate change and the final blow came when the Clovis people hunted the large herbivores to extinction, diminishing the carnivores' prey and leading to their extinction soon after.

If a combination of human migration and climate change was capable of causing such a catastrophic extinction then surely we have a lot to fear? As the human population grows from seven billion to a predicted nine billion by the year 2050, and our global climate warms at an unprecedented rate, could the next global mass extinction be just around the corner?

 SABRE-TOOTHED CAT

SCAN HERE

Gigantopithecus

Gigantopithecus blacki

THE DISCOVERY

In 1935 a distinguished German palaeoanthropologist, Professor Ralph von Koenigswald, was exploring the back streets of Hong Kong when he stumbled into a traditional Chinese apothecary shop. As his gaze travelled along the dusty shelves stacked full of trinkets and medicine bottles, his attention was drawn to a very unusual fossil. Upon closer inspection he recognised that it was a

◎ *Apothecary shops in China.*

fossilised tooth, similar to the molar tooth of a primate but much, much bigger. He was intrigued, knowing that it could not have belonged to any living species. For centuries, practitioners of traditional Chinese medicine had ground up these "dragon's teeth", meticulously dug up by farmers in caves across Southern China, for use as a cure to a wide number of ailments. For several years Von Koenigswald continued his search until he had unearthed three more similar giant teeth. He had discovered evidence of the existence of a giant ape, the largest primate ever to have lived and roamed our planet. He called the genus *Gigantopithecus*, meaning 'gigantic ape' and the species *blacki*.

Armed with his four molar teeth, Von Koenigswald was determined to find further fossilised remains of *Gigantopithecus blacki*. There were so many questions still to be answered. Where had it lived? How large could it have been? And when did it become extinct? Unfortunately, events beyond his control were to intervene and Von Koenigswald was enlisted to serve in World War II and subsequently taken prisoner by the Japanese in Java. All the while his precious collection of teeth, the only known specimens of the extinct ape *Gigantopithecus blacki*, was tucked away inside a milk bottle and buried in his friend's garden on the same island.

Did You Know?

Because of its immense size and weight, scientists believe *Gigantopithecus blacki* would have spent most of its time on the ground rather than in the trees.

○ *An illustration of a scene in North Vietnam 1.8 million years ago showing* Gigantopithecus, *the largest known primate, with* Homo erectus *to the left.*

WHERE DID GIGANTOPITHECUS LIVE?

After the war, Chinese palaeontologists wasted no time in taking up where Von Koenigswald had left off. Their search for the source of the "dragon teeth" took them to the remote Guangxi Province of Southern China, where the limestone landscape has been eroded and shaped into a maze of gorges, towering rocks, potholes and caves. In one of these caves they found over a thousand teeth belonging to *Gigantopithecus blacki* and, more significantly, they discovered three jawbones. One of the jawbones was significantly larger so they presumed it belonged to an adult male, while the other two they deduced belonged to a female and juvenile *Gigantopithecus blacki*.

The *Gigantopithecus's* native habitat, **South East Asia**

 GIGANTOPITHECUS

Even though this small locality in China has yielded the majority of *Gigantopithecus blacki* remains, fossils have also been found in Vietnam and Northern India so we can suppose that *Gigantopithecus blacki* was distributed across much of South East Asia. The fossils found in India have even been attributed to a smaller and more ancient species called *Gigantopithecus giganteus*.

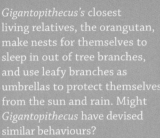

Gigantopithecus's closest living relatives, the orangutan, make nests for themselves to sleep in out of tree branches, and use leafy branches as umbrellas to protect themselves from the sun and rain. Might *Gigantopithecus* have devised similar behaviours?

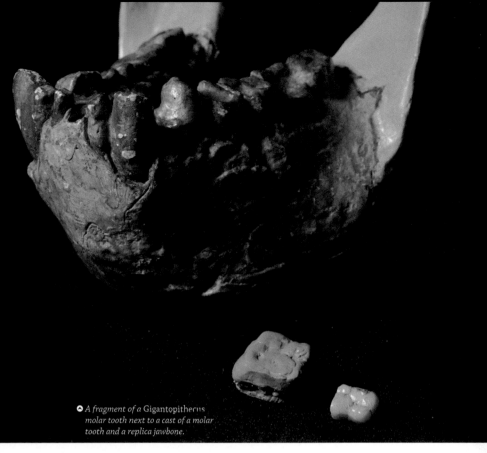

⬥ *A fragment of a* Gigantopithecus *molar tooth next to a cast of a molar tooth and a replica jawbone.*

PIECING TOGETHER THE CLUES

So what did *Gigantopithecus blacki* really look like?
It is very hard to reconstruct an extinct creature based on a meagre collection of fossilised jawbones and several hundred teeth. However, we do know that the closest living relative of *Gigantopithecus blacki* is the orangutan, found exclusively in the rainforests of Borneo and Sumatra in Indonesia. They spend their days high up in the forest canopy, feeding, resting and travelling, using their long arms to swing from tree to tree. Could the *Gigantopithecus blacki* have followed a similar lifestyle?

Based on the size of the molar teeth he found, Von Koeningswald knew it was a giant. Each *Gigantopithecus blacki* molar tooth dwarfs

that of a gorilla's, the largest ape alive today, and is up to six times as large as a human molar.

Using these teeth and jawbones, scientists have been able to estimate the size of *Gigantopithecus blacki*, scaling it up to an impressive three metres in height and a weight of over 500 kilograms. This really was a giant ape!

It is unlikely that an ape of this size could have lived high up in the trees like its cousins the orangutans. It would have been too heavy to be supported in the trees and surely at that size it would have had no predators to fear on the ground. So it is more likely that *Gigantopithecus blacki* lived on ground of its Southeast-Asian forest habitat, moving from site to site in search of food.

DIET

We can in fact infer quite a lot about the diet of *Gigantopithecus blacki* from its teeth. Firstly, the shape of its molar teeth are flattened with a thick layer of enamel, ideal for crushing hard foods. Secondly, its canines are short and blunt, rather than sharp and pointed like a carnivore, and allow side-to-side grinding. These features, combined with its deep set and robust jaw, would have made *Gigantopithecus blacki* perfectly adapted to feeding on a tough, fibrous, omnivorous diet.

If analysed under a microscope, some teeth even bare the remains of minute fragments of plants known as phytoliths. Their shape reveals they belonged to grasses, leading some to speculate that the diet of *Gigantopithecus blacki* included bamboo, abundant in that part of Asia, and the preferred diet of giant pandas today. However, patterns of microscopic pits and scratches on the grinding surfaces of the teeth are most similar to apes with omnivorous diets such as chimpanzees.

◉ *A giant panda,* Ailuropoda melanoleuca, *eating bamboo*

 GIGANTOPITHECUS

LOCOMOTION

Did the *Gigantopithecus blacki* live a sedentary lifestyle rather like the giant panda, a bamboo specialist? If it had a diverse diet like a chimpanzee, then it must have foraged widely through a large territory. Some scientists have speculated that it might even have walked on two feet rather than four, sparing its mobile shoulders and wrists from supporting its massive bulk, and freeing up its hands to grasp at or even carry food on the move.

HOW DID *GIGANTOPITHECUS* BECOME EXTINCT?

The most recent species of *Gigantopithecus* lived during the Pleistocene period, probably becoming extinct some 200,000 years ago. There are several interrelated factors that are thought to have led to its demise. One source of food, bamboo, is, for unknown reasons, prone to periodic die-offs, something that threatens giant pandas to this day. The final blow, however, might have been delivered by the hand of early man, who lived alongside *Gigantopithecus blacki* for many thousands of years following his migration into Southeast Asia about one million years ago. Humans may have directly hunted the *Gigantopithecus blacki* to extinction or may have exploited its bamboo for tools and other purposes. So perhaps environmental change had already weakened the *Gigantopithecus blacki* population and the arrival of humans was enough to tip the balance. In keeping with much of our scant knowledge of this creature, we will never know for sure what drove it to extinction.

A photograph of a Yeti Footprint with ice axe head taken by Eric Shipton, 1951.
Credit: Royal Geographical Society (with IBG)

THE MYTHS

For centuries reports of giant, hairy apes have captured our imagination and, in the twentieth century, they began to make headlines around the world. Even though cultures have always shared stories of mythical wildmen, it was in the 1950s that the Bigfoot and Sasquatch of the Pacific Northwest, and the Yeti or Abominable Snowman of the Himalayas entered popular culture. For some, the existence of *Gigantopithecus blacki* is simply the best explanation.

Perhaps the most famous evidence of a giant ape was found by a pair of British explorers. In 1951, the British climber Eric Shipton was coming to the end of his fifth expedition to Mount Everest when he and Dr. Michael Ward stumbled upon a huge set of footprints in the snow, "twelve inches long by five wide". To give an impression of scale Shipton placed his ice axe next to the print and took photographs of what were to become the most famous Yeti footprints of all.

The prints were discovered in the Menlung basin, on a glacier at a height of about 19,000 feet. Shipton and Ward followed the footprints for about a mile, remarking that, "these particular ones seemed to be very fresh, probably not more than 24 hours old." These were not the first tracks to be seen by early explorers and their Sherpas across the Himalayas. Sen Tenzing, his Nepalese guide, instantly recognized the prints and was convinced that the creature that produced the tracks were "Yetis or wild men" and that "he and a number of other Sherpas had seen one of them at a distance of about 25 yards at Thyangboche." Tenzing described the creature as "half man and half beast, with a tall pointed head, its body covered with reddish brown hair, but with a hairless face".

When Shipton's giant footprints began appearing on the front page of newspapers, the Yeti quickly became an international sensation. Could a small population of *Gigantopithecus* still exist in the remote foothills of the Himalayas? Many are still intrigued by the evidence, and expeditions are launched to this day in search of this elusive creature. With such a sparse fossil record *Gigantopithecus* was destined to remain something of a mythical creature, so its association with the legendary Abominable Snowman is not surprising. And yet the very existence of these fossils demonstrates that such an enormous ape did exist in the very recent past. Who knows what revelations may come to light in the years to come…

❍ *British mountain climber and explorer Eric Shipton (1907 - 1977)*

SCAN HERE

Ichthyosaur

Ichthyosaurus communis

Profile

Period:
They had become extinct 90 million years ago

Habitat:
Mesozoic Oceans

Size:
LENGTH
2 to 4 metres (6.5-13.1 ft.)
WEIGHT
163 kg (359 lb)
for a 2 metre (6.6 ft.) ichthyosaur
950 kg (2,090 lb)
for a 4 metre (13.1 ft.) ichthyosaur

Diet:
Belemnites (squid-like cephalopods with hooked arms and hard internal skeletons) as well as fish

THE DISCOVERY

At the beginning of the nineteenth century a very surprising fossil was found in the south of England, in the muddy cliffs near the sleepy seaside town of Lyme Regis. Perhaps the most fascinating part of this story was not the giant 'crocodile' that was discovered, but the fact that the discovery was made in part by a girl as young as 12 years old, Mary Anning. The impoverished Anning family had lived in the Dorset town for many years and Mary's father, Richard, was a cabinetmaker and amateur fossil hunter. When Richard died he left the family in huge debt, but did manage to pass on his skill and passion for fossil hunting. Mary and her brother Joseph proceeded to scrape together a living by selling their intriguing finds from a stall on the seafront to the many visitors to Lyme Regis each summer. Their shop became such a feature of the landscape that some people have speculated that Mary was the inspiration behind the well-known tongue-twister "She sells seashells on the seashore", which was written by Terry Sullivan in 1908.

> **MARY ANNING**
> **1799 - 1847**
>
> The famous fossilist was born here in a house on the site of Lyme Regis Museum. The house was her home & her fossil shop until 1826
>
> More about Mary Anning inside the Museum
>
> Mary Anning's house and shop drawn in 1842. It was demolished in 1889 to make way for the museum

© *Mary Anning plaque*

By the 1820s Mary Anning was running the family fossil-collecting business. Her keen eye and extraordinary ability to identify fossils made her an obvious choice to take on this role. At about this time the fossil collector Lieutenant-Colonel Thomas Birch visited the family and took pity on their financial situation. He held an auction of his fossil collection and donated the proceeds to the Anning family, declaring that they should not live in such "considerable difficulty" considering the contribution they had made to science.

● Beach at Lyme Regis.

The publicity generated by this sale consolidated Mary Anning's fame and, before long, the fossils that the Anning family had unearthed were being sought in earnest by scientists, museums and even the nobility. The near complete fossil Mary Anning and her brother found when she was just 12 years old was sold to Henry Hoste Henley of Colway Manor in Lyme for £23. Henley sent the fossil to London, where it was exhibited at William Bullock's Museum of Natural Curiosities. The specimen was later purchased by the British Museum (part of which became the Natural History Museum) and it greatly enhanced Mary Anning's reputation in scientific circles. It was named *Ichthyosaurus* – meaning 'fish-lizard' – by two scientists, Henry de la Beche and William Conybeare, in 1821.

● Mary Anning (1799-1847)

○ *'Duria Antiquior' by Henry de la Beche – 'ancient Dorset',*
based on fossils found by Mary Anning.

 ICHTHYOSAUR

THE AGE OF THE REPTILES

Over the course of her lifetime Mary Anning discovered numerous sensational finds including further ichthyosaur fossils, plesiosaurs and pterosaurs, all from the cliffs near Lyme Regis. Her discoveries were illustrated in a lithograph in 1830 by Henry de la Beche, which he called Duria Antiquior, or, "Ancient Dorset". It clearly depicts a world very different to the one we know now.

The ichthyosaurs were in fact reptiles, like crocodiles, lizards and snakes.

Ichthyosaurs originated in the Early Triassic, some 250 million years ago, and evolved into a huge variety of forms and sizes. They became the dominant predators of the Mesozoic ocean at the same time that the dinosaurs were ruling the land and the pterosaurs the skies. What exactly were ichthyosaurs? Well, this is a question that has puzzled many!

◐ *The fossils of several ichthyosaur species in the Natural History Museum, London.*

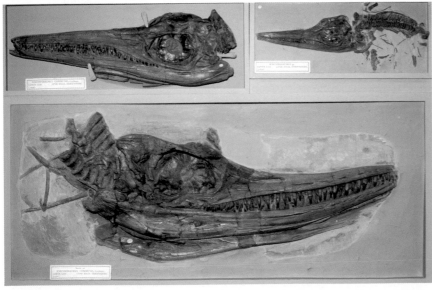

If you were to glance at the skeleton of an *Ichthyosaurus* you would not be alone in thinking it belonged to a fish. However, you would be wrong.

Brought to life with flesh and skin you might think that it was a marine mammal. Like dolphins, ichthyosaurs were air breathers, lacking gills and even giving birth to live young. But again, you would be wrong.

The ichthyosaurs were in fact reptiles, like crocodiles, lizards and snakes. Along with the plesiosaurs and mosasaurs they governed the Mesozoic seas. So it is not surprising that the Mesozoic era is often referred to as the age of the reptiles.

 ICHTHYOSAUR

CONVERGENT EVOLUTION

So how can three separate groups in the animal kingdom produce such strikingly similar creatures? The process of evolution will always select the most advantageous trait in terms of survival so, for any large animal swimming swiftly in the open sea, whether fish, mammal or reptile, this means a streamlined body shape. It's a process called convergent evolution.

Another compelling example is the convergent evolution of wings in the invertebrates (insects), mammals (bats), reptiles (pterosaurs) and birds. All four groups of animals have used their wings to fly and in doing so have exploited the skies. But these groups of animals are only very distantly related, each evolving the ability to fly completely independently.

There are some subtle differences between an ichthyosaur and a dolphin. The ichthyosaur has four fins rather than two and its tail is positioned vertically, rather like a tuna or mackerel, as opposed to horizontally like a dolphin or a whale. Tuna are amongst the fastest fish in the ocean today so can we presume that the ichthyosaur was built for speed? Or were they built to dive to great depths like a whale or perhaps perform acrobatics out of the water like a dolphin?

Well, there were over 100 species of ichthyosaur so it is quite possible that at least some of these were able to perform such tasks.

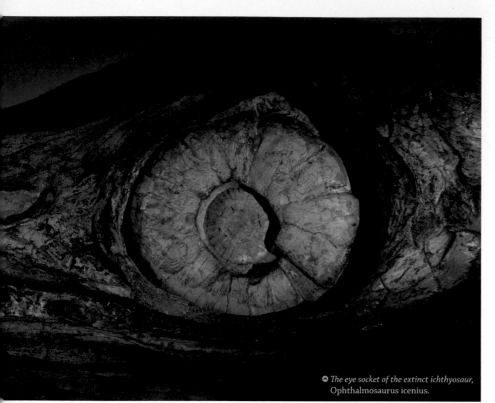

○ *The eye socket of the extinct ichthyosaur,*
Ophthalmosaurus icenius.

BENEATH THE WAVES

We can understand a surprising amount about the lifestyle of different ichthyosaur species by studying their skeletons.

It's hard to miss the prominent bony ring that marks the position of the eye socket in the skeleton of this *Ophthalmosaurus*. This bony sclerotic ring would have provided support for the very large eyeball. The eye of one ichthyosaur species, *Temnodontosaurus platyodon*, measured 264mm in diameter, making it one of the largest animal eyes ever recorded! Why would they need such large eyes? Well, not only were their eyes large but they were crammed full of photoreceptive cells, making the ichthyosaur's vision extremely sensitive at low light levels. This suggests that some species of ichthyosaur were capable of diving to the murky depths where light levels were very much reduced. Whales and other deep diving vertebrates are capable of flattening their lungs when they dive to minimise the effects of the increasing water pressure at depth. *Opthalmosaurus* might have had similar physiological adaptations that, coupled with the fact that reptiles require lower levels of oxygen than mammals of the same size, could mean they were potentially capable of diving to great depths and staying submerged for considerable periods of time.

Most ichthyosaurs had a long pointed jaw lined with rows of sharp, tightly-packed teeth. They were so precisely spaced that the upper and lower jaw could close with no gaps at all, making them quite a formidable weapon when snapped shut. Ichthyosaur skeletons have been found with the contents of their stomach preserved. Strange-looking, hooked structures frequently turn up which are now known to be the remains of squid-like creatures that lived in the Mesozoic ocean, the belemnites. Even though the ichthyosaurs probably would have feasted on a number of marine vertebrates, it seems that their

Did You Know?

The largest ichthyosaurian eye measured was 264 mm across, and belonged to a *Temnodontosaurus platyodon*. This is one of the largest eyes ever recorded for any animal.

⊙ *Colour printed illustration of ichthyosaurs jumping
by Heinrich Harder from* Tiere der Urwelt
Animals of the Prehistoric World, *1916.*

⊙ *Colour printed illustration of an Ichthyosaurus
communis by F. John from* Tiere der Urwelt
Animals of the Prehistoric World, *1910.*

Ichthyosaur
Stenopterygius quadriscissus (Quenstedt)
187 – 178 million years old
Lower Jurassic
Holzmaden, Baden-Württemberg, Germany

R5463 Replica purchased from Stuttgart Museum in 1928

This female ichthyosaur has the broken up skeletons of three unborn young inside her body. Notice the fourth baby ichthyosaur just beneath the mother's tail. This suggests it was born tail-first just as its mother died.

preferred food was usually squid-like, just like many species of whale today and a type of diet that is common amongst deep divers. One theory for this preference is that squid at deeper depths are more sluggish and present an easier meal choice than squid nearer the surface. Evidence from the structure of the bones in their braincase and ear suggests that the ichthyosaurs did not use echolocation to hunt as dolphins do today. Instead they would have relied on their sharp teeth and acute vision to catch their squid-like prey.

 ICHTHYOSAUR

As with modern marine mammals, the ichthyosaurs were air-breathers, frequently swimming to the surface to take a breath. Modern spinner dolphins are famous for their playful acrobatics, swimming at speed through the water, breaking the surface and spinning for several metres before crashing back beneath the waves. Perhaps their splashing is a way of communicating with each other, or maybe they are just jumping high to get a better view of the horizon. We will never know for sure. Could an ichthyosaur have jumped out of the water in the same way as a spinner dolphin? We know they could swim at high speeds so there seems no reason why an ichthyosaur couldn't generate enough power with its strong tail to propel itself out of the water. So perhaps some species of ichthyosaur would indeed have rivaled a modern dolphin in acrobatic skills.

SCAN HERE

Archaeopteryx

Archaeopteryx lithographica

AN EXTREMELY VALUABLE DISCOVERY

Once upon a time, some 150 million years ago, a shallow lagoon became cut off from the ocean that had created it. As temperatures soared the water began to evaporate until all that was left was an increasingly salty and stagnant body of water. Although the surface waters still teemed with life, after death their bodies sank to the depths where few animals lived, so their skeletons were hardly disturbed.

Over many millions of years, the sediments accumulating at the bottom of this lagoon turned into something very useful – limestone – and the local people in Bavaria, Germany, where this lagoon once existed, mine this limestone for floor and roof tiles to this day. In the process they regularly uncover spectacular fossils of complete skeletons, some even with soft tissue preserved, which they sell to scientists and tourists.

This quarry has provided a window into the world of the Late Jurassic, with over 600 species having been discovered. Jellyfish, squid, horseshoe crabs, ammonites and fish all thrived within the lagoon. Fossils of predatory fish and pterosaurs with their stomach contents preserved, and even the fossil of a fish in the process of swallowing another, allow us a sneak peak at the lives these animals led, what they ate and how they died. As well as marine crocodiles and turtles, the skeletons of three dinosaurs, *Compsognathus*, *Juravenator* and *Sciurumimus* have also been found.

Profile

Period:
They had become extinct 150 million years ago

Habitat:
Bavaria, Germany.

Size:

HEIGHT
0.3 metres (1 ft.)

LENGTH
Up to 50 cm (1.6 ft.)

WEIGHT
0.8 - 1.0 kg (1.8 - 2.2 lb)

Diet:
Insects

ARCHAEOPTERYX

One of the most famous fossils ever discovered was unearthed in the Solnhofen limestones of Germany in 1861. Christian Erich Hermann von Meyer, a distinguished palaeontologist of the time, was given the fossil of a blackish feather, pressed between two limestone slabs.

He instantly recognised its asymmetric form and deduced that it must have been a wing feather much like those found on modern birds. Based on this single feather, Meyer called the creature it had come from *Archaeopteryx lithographica*, meaning "ancient wing". It was just six weeks later that Meyer announced the discovery of a feathered skeleton of *Archaeopteryx lithographica*, also from the limestone quarries of Solnhofen.

These discoveries created a huge amount of confusion amongst palaeontologists in Germany. It had the feathers of a bird, but the teeth, claws and long bony tail of a reptile. There was no doubt in Meyer's mind that the skeleton and feather belonged to a bird. However, many disagreed, believing it was a pterosaur (flying reptile) with feathers. One scientist even wrote that it was a fake and that the feathers had been etched onto the limestone, artificially engraved to appear as a natural imprint.

Word of these remarkable discoveries quickly reached Richard Owen, then the superintendent of the natural history department of the British Museum, and he proceeded to purchase the 'feathered fossil', amongst others, for the vast sum of £700. In 1862 this was a considerable amount of money and the museum had to allocate £450 from its budget for the current year and £250 from the following year's budget.

On October 1st, 1862, the valuable fossil arrived in London, much to the discontent of German scientists. An expert anatomist, Owen quickly set to work studying the fossil, describing the species shortly afterwards as a long-tailed bird and, at about 150 million years old, it was by far the oldest bird ever discovered. He presumed the reptilian features on the slab of limestone must be the remains of a fish that had died alongside it. However, Owen had failed to realise just how important *Archaeopteryx* really was.

The *Archaeopteryx's* native habitat,
Bavaria, Germany

The London specimen, *Archaeopteryx lithographica*, one of only 10 fossils of this animal ever discovered.

COULD *ARCHAEOPTERYX* FLY?

Recent dinosaur fossils discovered in China have also been found to have feathers, but scientists believe that their feathers were adapted for display (attracting a mate) or for warmth. So, were the feathers of *Archaeopteryx* actually adapted for flying? Back in 1861 Meyer recognised the asymmetric form of the *Archaeopteryx* feathers as something seen in the flight feathers of modern birds. It is this asymmetric shape that makes the flight feathers of birds aerodynamic. But this alone is not enough evidence to suppose *Archaeopteryx* could fly. Perhaps, rather than flapping its feathers like a modern bird, the *Archaeopteryx* used its stiff, aerodynamic feathers to glide from the treetops, saving precious energy?

There is, however, another clue in the fossil slab of the London specimen, the first *Archaeopteryx* ever discovered. The brains of birds tend to fit snuggly inside their protective skulls so scientists at the Natural History Museum, London were able to scan the skull and reveal the intricate impressions left by its brain.

What they discovered was that the brain of the *Archaeopteryx* had lobes large enough to process vast amounts of sensory information; the sort of information required for balance and coordination in active flight. Whilst it was probably not an expert flier, it seems likely that *Archaeopteryx* was capable of using its feathered wings for flapping flight, allowing it, alongside pterosaurs, to reign over the Jurassic skies.

ARCHAEOPTERYX – THE HUNTER

If *Archaeopteryx* was capable of flapping flight then this would have freed up its large grasping claws for other uses. Early palaeontologists thought that it might have used its claws for grasping fish on the wing as it swooped low over the coastal lagoon, in the same way as a pterosaur. However, only 10 *Archaeopteryx* fossils have ever been recovered from the Solnhofen limestone quarry compared with hundreds of pterosaur fossils, suggesting that *Archaeopteryx* was not a coastal bird. Also, it lacked the aerodynamic skill required to fly in control over water and hunt. More likely it lived inland, some distance from the coastline, and the few fossilised skeletons that have been uncovered were already dead when they were swept into the lagoon. Perhaps *Archaeopteryx* used its large claws to grip branches and bark during climbing, to escape from predators or to find a perch whilst it surveyed the landscape for a tasty meal.

The beak shapes of modern birds give away their preferred diet, with the beaks of seed eaters easy to distinguish from those of insect eaters or from birds of prey. *Archaeopteryx* lacked a horny beak, like modern birds, and instead had a snout lined with a series of serrated teeth, similar to a carnivorous dinosaur. The rich fossil record of Solnhofen suggests that there was an abundance of land insects at the time, so it seems likely that *Archaeopteryx* used its teeth to trap and crush the hard exoskeletons of a variety of different insects. *Archaeopteryx* was a hunter.

SCAN HERE

Iguanodon

Iguanodon bernissartensis

THE DISCOVERY

⊙ *Original* Iguanodon *tooth found by Dr. and Mrs. Mantell.*

At about the same time that Mary Anning was digging up the fossils of marine reptiles along the Dorset coastline, another amateur fossil hunter made something of a chance discovery which was to prove to be just as significant. The story goes that in 1822 Mary Ann Mantell, the wife of a country doctor Gideon Mantell, noticed something glinting in a pile of rubble by the side of the road in Sussex whilst she waited for her husband to finish a house call. She stepped down from their carriage to take a closer look and picked up two rocks with some sort of fossils embedded in them. When Gideon emerged from his appointment, Mary Ann showed him her find and, being an enthusiastic fossil collector and passionate geologist, he immediately recognised that they were fossilised teeth.

Profile

Period:

Iguanodon had become extinct 110 million years ago

Habitat:

United Kingdom, Germany, France, Spain, Belgium

Size:

HEIGHT/LENGTH
Iguanodon grew to a length of up to 10m and a height of 3-5m - it was almost the size of a house!

WEIGHT
4,000 Kg – 5,000 Kg (4-5 Tonnes)

Diet:

Tough fibrous plant material

Plate III.

1

3

2

5

4

F. Pollard lith.

Printed by Graf & Soret

London, Published by Longman & Co.

● *Gideon Mantell (1790 - 1852)*

● *Mary Ann Mantell (1799 - 1847)*

A FORMIDABLE TEAM

When Gideon Mantell published a description of this discovery it was Mary Ann who provided the many exquisite pen and ink sketches that filled its pages, including those of the teeth she had found. Professionally it seems they made quite a formidable team, but the same could not be said for their marriage. Mary Ann became more and more exasperated by Gideon's unending devotion to his work and so finally, feeling utterly neglected, she made a very brave decision and divorced him in 1839.

◀ *The "Horn of the Iguanodon" from*
The Geology of the South East of England
by Gideon Mantell, 1833.
Credit: Science Photo Library

Quarry scene, Tilgate Forest, from the
Geology of Sussex (1827) by G. A. Mantell.

DIGGING DEEPER

Gideon Mantell realised that the fossils were teeth but could not
identify which creature they belonged to. He painstakingly traced
the source of the rock in which the fossils were embedded to a quarry
in Whiteman's Green, Cuckfield, Sussex. He set the quarrymen
the challenge of uncovering more fossils for a cash reward and,
sure enough, it wasn't long before they uncovered further remains,
including more teeth.

A keen geologist, he knew from the age of the surrounding rock that
the mysterious creature to which the teeth belonged must have lived

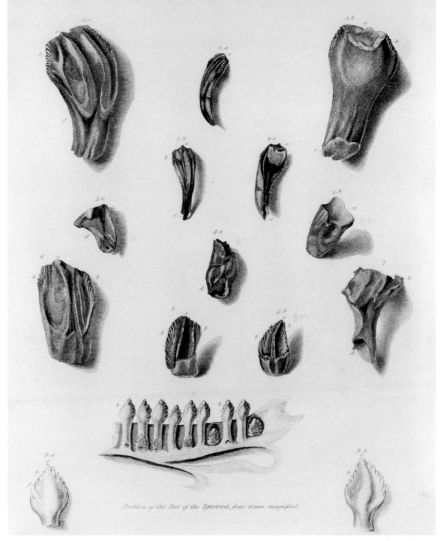

Drawings by palaeontologist Gideon Mantell (1790-1852) showing the Iguanodon *fossil teeth he discovered.*

in the Lower Cretaceous age, which we now know was about 135 million years ago. Still bemused as to their identity, he sent the teeth for further inspection. A prominent scientist, William Buckland, professor of geology at Oxford University at the time, dismissed Mantell, believing the teeth were those of a fish.

Unperturbed, Mantell sent the teeth off to Paris with his trusted friend and fellow geologist Charles Lyell. At a party one evening Lyell presented the teeth to the famous French anatomist Baron Georges Cuvier. He also rejected them, claiming they were the teeth of a rhinoceros, and advised Mantell to pursue the matter no further.

Mantell was dismayed but by no means dissuaded from continuing with his quest. He made the journey to London to visit the Royal College of Surgeons, where an anatomist, Samuel Stutchbury, showed him the skeleton of an iguana recently collected in the West Indies by none other than Charles Darwin. Mantell immediately recognised that his teeth were identical to those of the iguana, just much larger, and in a "Eureka!" moment deduced that, about 135 million years ago, a giant, plant-eating reptile must have roamed across the south of England. He estimated it must have been up to 60 feet in length and he called it *Iguanodon*, meaning "iguana tooth".

RECONSTRUCTING THE *IGUANODON*

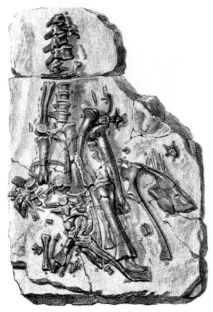

The famous 'Mantell piece', a rock slab containing the most complete set of articulated dinosaur bones discovered at the time.

In 1834 Mantell heard about a significant discovery of bones in a pit in Maidstone, Kent. Unfortunately the site was dynamited before he arrived, but there still remained one large slab with several bones embedded in it. Mantell was unable to pay the hefty £25 price tag demanded by the quarry owner, but his friends clubbed together and bought the rock for him. The Maidstone slab, or "Mantell piece" as it became more commonly known, is now on permanent display in the Natural History Museum, London.

Mantell set about the task of trying to reconstruct the *Iguanodon* based on this slab of rock and the many other isolated bones he had recovered from Cuckfield and elsewhere. His initial drawings showed a creature resembling a modern iguana, standing on four legs. Curiously he placed a "horn" on the creature's snout, rather like that of a rhinoceros.

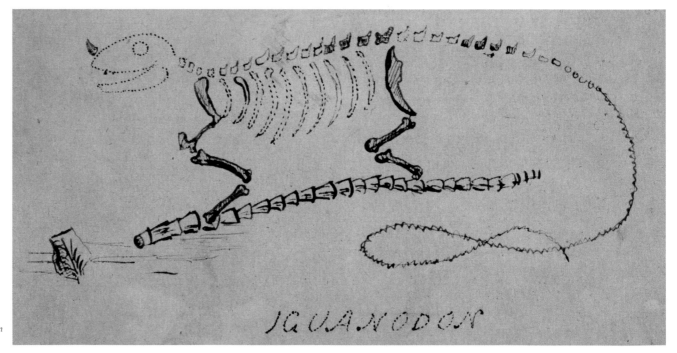

Iguanodon reconstruction by Gideon Mantell

A CLASS OF THEIR OWN

A couple of years after he had dismissed Mantell's teeth as belonging to a fish, the eccentric Professor Buckland formally described the jaw of an animal that had been sitting gathering dust in the University of Oxford's Museum for many years. He recognised that it too belonged to a giant reptile and he called it *Megalosaurus*.

Later, Professor Richard Owen also began working on the specimens initially described by Buckland and Mantell as well as other bones sent to him from quarries all over southern England. Owen decided that the giant reptilian fossils of *Iguanodon*, *Megalosaurus* and a third,

Hylaeosaurus (also discovered by Mantell), were so unlike any creatures ever seen before that they should be placed in a reptile group all of their own. So, in 1842, he did just that, calling them the "dinosaurs", meaning "terrible lizards".

Having coined the term "dinosaur", Owen instantly grabbed the headlines. Much to the irritation of Mantell, Owen accepted the glory for the discovery of the dinosaurs, a title that really should have been awarded to Mantell. To Mantell, Owen's behaviour was "unworthy piracy" and he was horrified that "a man of so much talent should be so dastardly and envious".

A MOST UNUSUAL INVITATION

Gideon Mantell had made a number of early discoveries, but Richard Owen had given the dinosaurs legendary status. Owen worked with the sculptor Benjamin Waterhouse Hawkins to produce some life-size reconstructions of dinosaurs for the public to enjoy at the Great Exhibition of 1851.

Following the Great Exhibition, the Crystal Palace was moved to Sydenham Hill in South London and, as part of the restoration, Hawkins was commissioned to fill the dinosaur park with 33 models of dinosaurs and extinct creatures. Among the models was a pair of *Iguanodon*, still posed on four legs with the curious rhinoceros-like horn on their nose, but they were much stockier and less lizard-like than those reconstructed by Mantell.

To launch the unveiling of the dinosaur models in Crystal Palace Park, Owen held a dinner on New Year's Eve, 1853. But this was no ordinary dinner! Owen hosted a banquet for 20 people and held it in the grounds of the park inside the mold used to build the *Iguanodon* models.

These concrete models transfixed the Victorian people and for the next 25 years it was this image of the dinosaurs that stuck.

◐ Iguanodon *reconstructions in Crystal Palace Park*

◖ *Victorian invitation and menu for dinner at Crystal Palace (New Year's Eve 1853)*

 IGUANODON

A MORE MODERN INTERPRETATION

Not everyone was convinced that Owen's interpretation of *Iguanodon*, standing in pride of place in what is now Crystal Palace Park, was the correct one.

❏ *Thomas Henry Huxley (1825-1895)*

In 1854, Samuel Beckles had stumbled across several three-toed footprints in the Wealden rocks of the Isle of Wight. He was sure that the footprints could have belonged to a dinosaur but noticed the similarities with the familiar footprint of a bird. Shortly afterwards Beckles found the leg bone of an *Iguanodon* which was distinctively three-toed and was evidence in his mind that the prints had been made by a dinosaur.

Thomas Huxley, a prominent scientist of the time, was also convinced the footprints belonged to *Iguanodon*, suggesting that its hind legs were sufficiently strong to support its entire weight – he believed that *Iguanodon* was bipedal, capable of standing on two feet rather than four. His belief was strengthened in the 1880s when whole skeletons were unearthed. None were more spectacular than the discovery made by some coalminers in Belgium. Having dug down over 300 metres they struck against what they believed to be petrified wood. They continued to dig until they realised they had discovered the near complete skeleton of an *Iguanodon* and, more significantly, not just one skeleton. They found the fossilised remains of 31, fully-grown, adult *Iguanodon* that had perished in this one spot.

The skeletons were excavated and reconstructed in the only building large enough to hold such a creature in a bipedal stance – a church – before being moved to a museum in Brussels where they still stand to this day.

And what about that 'horn'? If the *Iguanodon* had roamed the Cretaceous on two legs then this would have freed up its arms for performing a number of possible tasks. Other discoveries of more complete skeletons have shown that the spike-like bone was not a 'horn' at all. In fact it was a thumb spike, a very useful defensive weapon.

This upright posture of the *Iguanodon* prevailed for nearly 100 years. However, in the 1980s scientists looked more closely at the *Iguanodon* in the dinosaur gallery at Natural History Museum. They realised that it had had its tail broken to allow it to stand upright and maintain that bipedal pose!

So, once again, our understanding of this dinosaur was turned on its head. Scientists now believe that the *Iguanodon* did walk on four legs as Mantell had first suggested, using its tail as a counterbalance. However, it might also have been able to walk on two legs from time to time with some experts speculating that it walked on two legs as a juvenile and on four as it aged and its tendons hardened to bone. One thing is for sure, in the world of palaeontology new discoveries are made on a daily basis and so our understanding of how these creatures might have appeared in life is constantly being updated.

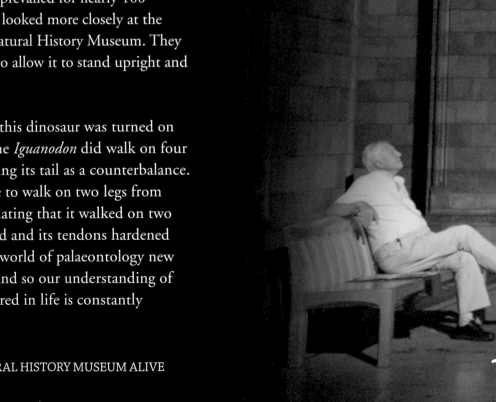

SCAN HERE

Period:

They had become extinct 150 million years ago

Habitat:

Found in western North America, its habitat included large rivers, open forest and vast plains.

Size:

HEIGHT
Up to 4 metres (13 ft) at the shoulder, but could stand on its back legs and crane its neck to a height of 10 metres (33 ft)

LENGTH
Up to 33 metres (108 ft)

WEIGHT
10-15 tonnes (11-17 tons)

Diet:

Soft leaves of conifers, gingkos, seed ferns, cycads, bennettitaleans, ferns, club mosses, and horsetails

Dippy

Diplodocus carnegii

BONE WARS

Richard Owen coined the term "dinosaur" in 1842, to describe the spectacular giant reptiles being dug up across southern England and Europe and, before long, news of these discoveries was being announced across the world. At about the same time, early settlers in North America began to head West in their thousands, in search of greener pastures. As they began to cultivate the land and build railways they stumbled upon some sensational fossils of their own. This sparked an intense competition as scientists fought to recover and identify the finest dinosaur skeletons. If a team of bone collectors chanced upon a rival team at work, fistfights and even gun battles could ensue.

One of the most avid collectors was Professor Othniel C. Marsh from Yale University. In 1878, he described a dinosaur from the backbones, hip, hind leg and tail bones unearthed in Colorado. He noticed that some of the dinosaur's tail bones, known as the chevrons, had an unusual shape. They were split into forward and backward projecting prongs and so he called the dinosaur *Diplodocus*, meaning "Double Beam".

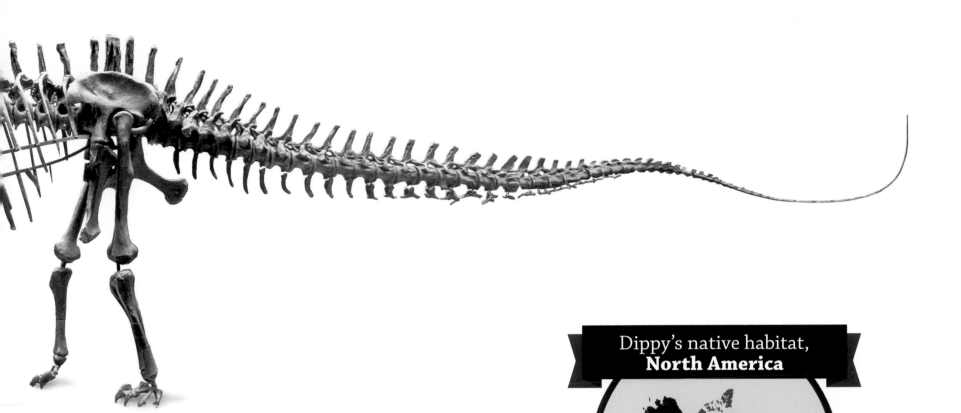

Dippy's native habitat, North America

Dippy lived about 157 to 150 million years ago and, at 26 metres, was one of the longest and largest land animals ever to walk the Earth.

◀ *First discovery of the long hind leg of the dinosaur Diplodocus by Henry Fairfield Osborn in 1898 at Bone Cabin Quarry in Wyoming, America.*

WHAT KINGS WANT THEY GET

Towards the end of 1898 the newspapers in New York City were awash with stories of the discovery of a near complete skeleton of an animal of unimaginable scale, "120,000 pounds in weight and 130 feet long", in the badlands near Sheep Creek, Wyoming. Scottish-born Andrew Carnegie, an extremely wealthy businessman and generous philanthropist, had just opened the Carnegie Museum in Pittsburgh, U.S.A. and he sent his newly appointed director, William Holland, to go and retrieve the skeleton. As it turned out, it was not quite as colossal as the newspapers had made out, but still the discovery was of one of the largest dinosaurs then known to science, and Holland identified that it was the skeleton of a *Diplodocus*. The bones were packed up and transported by train to Pittsburgh where began the process of preparing them for display. Carnegie and Holland enlisted the help of John Hatcher, a prominent palaeontologist of the time, to oversee this painstaking process.

◉ *Andrew Carnegie (1835 - 1919)*

Hatcher noticed several small differences between his bones and those of other *Diplodocus* bones and so he described a new species and called it *Diplodocus carnegii* after his patron, Andrew Carnegie. Hatcher compiled a detailed scientific paper to describe every aspect of the dinosaur and he included exquisite illustrations of the *Diplodocus carnegii* skeleton. One of these illustrations, of the complete *Diplodocus carnegii* skeleton reconstructed, was

hanging on the wall of Andrew Carnegie's Skibo Castle in Scotland in 1902 when a very important guest paid a visit.

◉ *King Edward VII (1841–1910)*

Edward VII was so impressed by the illustration that he enquired as to whether he could get hold of a *Diplodocus* skeleton himself. Carnegie sent the request on to Holland who replied that it was unlikely they would find another such complete skeleton, but would a plaster replica be sufficient? In those days, what kings wanted, they got, and Carnegie paid a considerable sum to make Edward VII's wish come true. A team of three expert plasterers were drafted in from Italy and they set to work making Plaster of Paris replicas of every bone before painting them black. In a year and a half they created 292 plaster bones that were shipped to London in 36 packing crates!

At one o'clock in the afternoon on Friday, 12th May, 1905, Andrew Carnegie officially unveiled the replica of *Diplodocus carnegii* to some 200 people squeezed into the Reptile Gallery of the Natural History Museum in London. The replica skeleton was 84 feet long and 15 feet high and it was the first full-sized skeleton of a sauropod dinosaur to be put on display anywhere in the world. It is not hard to imagine what a sensation it caused!

In 1979, the *Diplodocus carnegii* skeleton, or Dippy as it is affectionately called, was moved to a place of honour in the Central Hall and it is still a favourite with visitors to this day.

◐ Dippy being being unveiled in the
Natural History Museum, London, in 1905.

◐ Cartoon illustration from 1905, showing
how the new Diplodocus cast might be used
in the Natural History Museum.

SCRAPS
June 3, 1905.

86

STICKS, UMBRELLAS
PARASOLS COATS
WRAPS &c SHOULD
BE LEFT HERE

PARCELS
MAY BE LEFT
HERE

How the Diplodocus Skeleton might be made useful as well as ornamental. Suggestion gratis to the Museum authorities.

MAY 16, 1905.

THE WESTMINSTER GAZETTE.

◁ *Illustration of an aquatic Diplodocus.*

BRINGING DIPPY TO LIFE

▷ *Illustration of a Diplodocus by Heinrich Harder from* Tiere der Urwelt Animals of the Prehistoric World, *1916, Hamburg.*

Dippy belongs to a group of dinosaurs called sauropods. They are characterised by their extremely long necks and tails, a feature, amongst others, which led to a huge amount of confusion and speculation when it was discovered.

In 1908, Oliver Hay suggested that the legs of a *Diplodocus* must have splayed out like those of a crocodile. He believed that their small limbs would not have been able to support their weight so they would have dragged their bellies through the Jurassic mud, like lizards or crocodiles. William Holland rebuffed this theory, realising that the way the back and hip bones of a *Diplodocus* were positioned meant that their legs were likely to be directly under their body, more like an elephant.

Skull of a Diplodocus *dinosaur.*

However, Holland, along with many others, believed that even with its legs positioned below its body, a *Diplodocus* could not have been terrestrial. Surely no 20-tonne dinosaur would have been able to support such weight on land?

If *Diplodocus* was amphibious then the water would act to support its vast body size, rather like a blue whale. Aspects of its skeleton provided further evidence for this aquatic lifestyle. The clawed feet of a *Diplodocus* were thought to be an adaptation to give traction on muddy lake floors, and its peg-like teeth were ideal for browsing on soft aquatic vegetation. Air cavities in their vertebrae might have acted like buoys, helping them to stay afloat when in deep water.

Did You Know?

Dippy had about 40 working teeth at any one time, all of which were pointing slightly forward giving her a very goofy expression. These teeth – peg-like and arranged with spaces between them like the teeth of a comb - may have been ideally suited to stripping foliage from branches rather than grazing the ground. Each of these teeth was actually replaced every 35 days!

The most conclusive evidence for the aquatic lifestyle of a *Diplodocus*, however, was a large hole on the top of its skull. If you were to spend your entire life in the water, then surely a blow-hole cavity like this would make a lot of sense? As for that long neck, they presumed that a *Diplodocus* would have used it like a snorkel!

More recent research has shown that in fact these theories were entirely incorrect. Their legs were strong, acting like pillars, and would have been more than capable of holding up their body on land. The discovery of fossilised *Diplodocus* footprints is evidence that they did in fact live on land. The idea that a *Diplodocus* would walk along the floor of a lake with its neck acting like a snorkel is unlikely. The forces acting on its body at such a depth would have made drawing air into its lungs impossible. And what about the hole on the top of its skull? In fact it seems more likely that it was part of an elaborate nasal system and that its nostrils would have been positioned further forward on its skull.

So if Dippy didn't use its long neck as a snorkel then what was it used for? Over the years scientists have proposed many theories for the function of the long neck in sauropod dinosaurs. Perhaps they evolved as a signal to members of the opposite sex? Or, perhaps they were used by males as a weapon, swinging their long necks at would-be-attackers in the same way that giraffes do. Some even proposed that their long necks were a way of controlling their body temperature. With such a large surface area they thought that their necks might have helped these huge dinosaurs to cool down.

We know that Dippy was a herbivore so it seems most likely that it used its long neck for browsing. It could sweep its neck along the ground in search of food and reach up into the highest trees to get at the juiciest vegetation.

So we now know how Dippy was likely to hold its long neck, but why did Dippy need such a long tail? Advanced computer modelling programs have shown that Dippy could whip its tail at supersonic speeds, with the very tip of the tail moving as fast as a bull-whip – almost 800 mph! So perhaps it used its tail as a weapon against predators. In addition, scientists now think that Dippy might have used its tail as a counter-balance for its long neck and as a prop, allowing it to rear up on its back legs to browse the very highest branches. If Dippy was to rear up in this way it would have been able to reach as high as 10 metres!

Did You Know?

Dippy could rear up onto her hind legs using her tail for support, reaching as high as 10 metres - more than twice the height of a double-decker bus!

With an overall weight of 15 tonnes Dippy weighed as much as a fully loaded school bus – with 84 pupils inside!

PUZZLING PIECES

Locked away in a store room of the Natural History Museum is a very special specimen that has provided an insight into how the sauropod dinosaurs might have lived out the first few years of their lives.

It is an egg belonging, scientists presume but cannot prove, to a sauropod dinosaur like Dippy. Significantly, this was one of the first dinosaur eggs ever discovered, and the largest. At about 30 centimetres in diameter, and with a volume of about half a gallon, it is twice the size of an ostrich egg!

Since the first dinosaur eggs were discovered, many more have been unearthed across the world. It seems that a female sauropod dinosaur would lay several clutches of 10 or so eggs in soft ground. Then she would abandon the nest to re-join her herd. When the young sauropod was large enough, it would crack out of its shell using a specially modified sharp tooth – an egg tooth.

The sauropodlets would have hatched at an impressive one metre in length, but they then had a lot of growing to do. They probably lived out their first few years sheltered in the forest undergrowth whilst they ate an estimated 2 kilograms of vegetation a day!

An egg found near to the bones of the sauropod dinosaur, Hypselosaurus.

SCAN HERE

Bringing The Creatures Back To Life

This book is a complement to the 90-minute film, David Attenborough's Natural History Museum Alive 3D, produced by Colossus Productions for Sky 3D with the Natural History Museum, London. This project grew out of an ongoing 3D production partnership between David Attenborough, Sky 3D and Atlantic productions to produce 3D films. The idea for the project first came when we were filming a sequence at the Museum recreating early pterosaurs emerging from fossils for a sequence in Flying Monsters 3D with David Attenborough. For our sixth production, we were looking for a film which would work well for all ages at Christmas time. David has had a long association with the Natural History Museum, having first been fascinated by it as an 8-year-old child. From this, the project grew into the idea of David alone in the Museum at night, visiting some of his favourite extinct creatures which come back to life. The Museum provided the scientific expertise we needed for the creatures, top computer graphics houses brought the creatures back to life and a world class production team made David's script a reality. We hope this film will allow a whole new generation to enjoy the Museum. There is also an accompanying app which, along with this book, will allow you to continue your own journey.

Anthony Geffen
Producer and CEO, Colossus Productions

NATURAL HISTORY MUSEUM ALIVE 3D breaks new ground as the visual effects team bring the most iconic extinct creatures in the Museum back to life, allowing legendary broadcaster David Attenborough to come face-to-face with them. Though the production team and David have collaborated on award-winning CGI projects in the past, never before have they been on this scale and with such ambitions towards photo-realism and scientific accuracy.

The remarkable history of these incredible extinct animals, as told in this book, and the continuing scientific analysis of their remains can tell us a great deal about how they may have looked and behaved in life. But the challenge we faced for this acclaimed film was to recreate them as entirely believable, photo-realistic animals using CGI (computer generated imagery). A dozen creatures, encompassing hundreds of millions of years of natural history, were selected by David to feature in the film. Each had a personal significance and great stories...but in addition they also set unique challenges for the visual effects

team. There were feathers and fur to simulate, needing to move and interact convincingly with the body, underwater creatures required to swim gracefully through thin air and muscle systems to be specially designed for our giant ground sloth to dig straight into the museum floor. The decision was made to carve out the creatures and give them to different animation studios that had unique specialisms. Fido, based in Sweden, had worked with us before on the award-winning *Flying Monsters 3D with David Attenborough*, but it was their shots for a recent commercial, featuring a bird of prey, that dropped jaws in terms of sheer realism and secured them four of the film's feathery creatures: the dodo, moa, *Archaeopteryx* and the *Harpagornis*. Jellyfish Pictures, in London's Soho, appropriately took the marine reptile Ichthyosaur, and Milk was given the film's furry beasts, *Gigantopithecus* and *Glossotherium*. The dinosaurs and skeletal creatures went to longtime collaborators ZOO and CVFX. All these teams were managed by VFX Supervisor James Prosser who had to ensure continuity of style across the whole film.

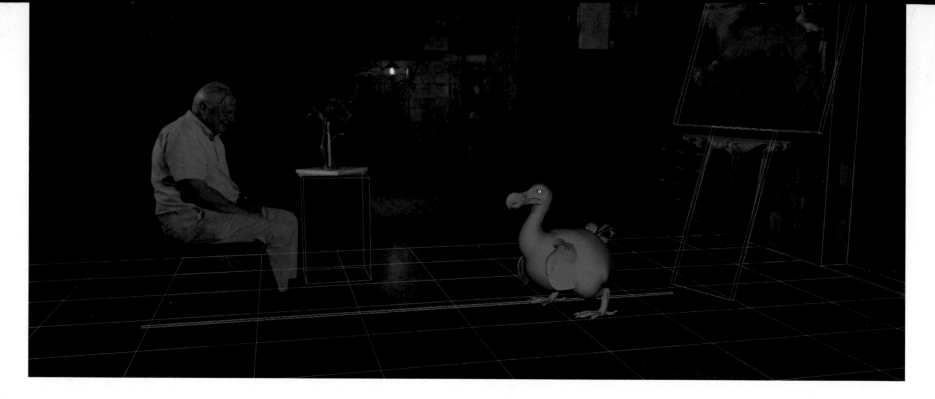

Research is paramount when bringing a creature to life in CGI. Talking to leading experts, reading detailed books on bio-mechanics, and studying similar creatures that are alive in the natural world are all essential. But there comes a time when you have to sit down and actually build it. This job falls to the modeller and they have to start with a ball of virtual clay in the computer software much like a sculptor does in the real world. These are the crude first steps: general body shape, scale and proportions. And in our case it had to match exactly the fossil or skeleton from which the creature magically emerges within the Museum.

Once this initial model of the creature was complete there began a regular dialogue with the Museum curators and world's leading experts. This continued every step of the way. Initial storyboards and animations throw up questions about scale, posture, locomotion – the actual physics of the creature. Look development lets you see the more realistic-looking finish of the creatures, with skin textures, fur, feathers or scales applied. Again, there was another chance to feedback here. With two of our animals having been indigenous to New Zealand we reached out, with the museum's guidance, to the world expert who was based there and remotely addressed every tiny detail of appearance and behaviour. David Attenborough too was part of the review process at all times – which he found endlessly fascinating.

Amazingly, in bringing these creatures back to life for this film, it has enhanced our understanding of them and even challenged some long held beliefs. Seeing the dodo with fluffier feathers, different colourings, posed more upright and behaving aggressively, provides a marked contrast to its usual fat, clumsy depiction; whilst the preposterous canines of *Smilodon*, the sabre-toothed cat, often the cause of much discussion in scientific circles, were really put to the test when we had to animate a bite. With the restrictions of just how wide it was able to open its jaws, the sheer size of the teeth and the dimensions of the prey's neck, you get an idea of just how difficult it must have been to use those dagger-like weapons effectively.

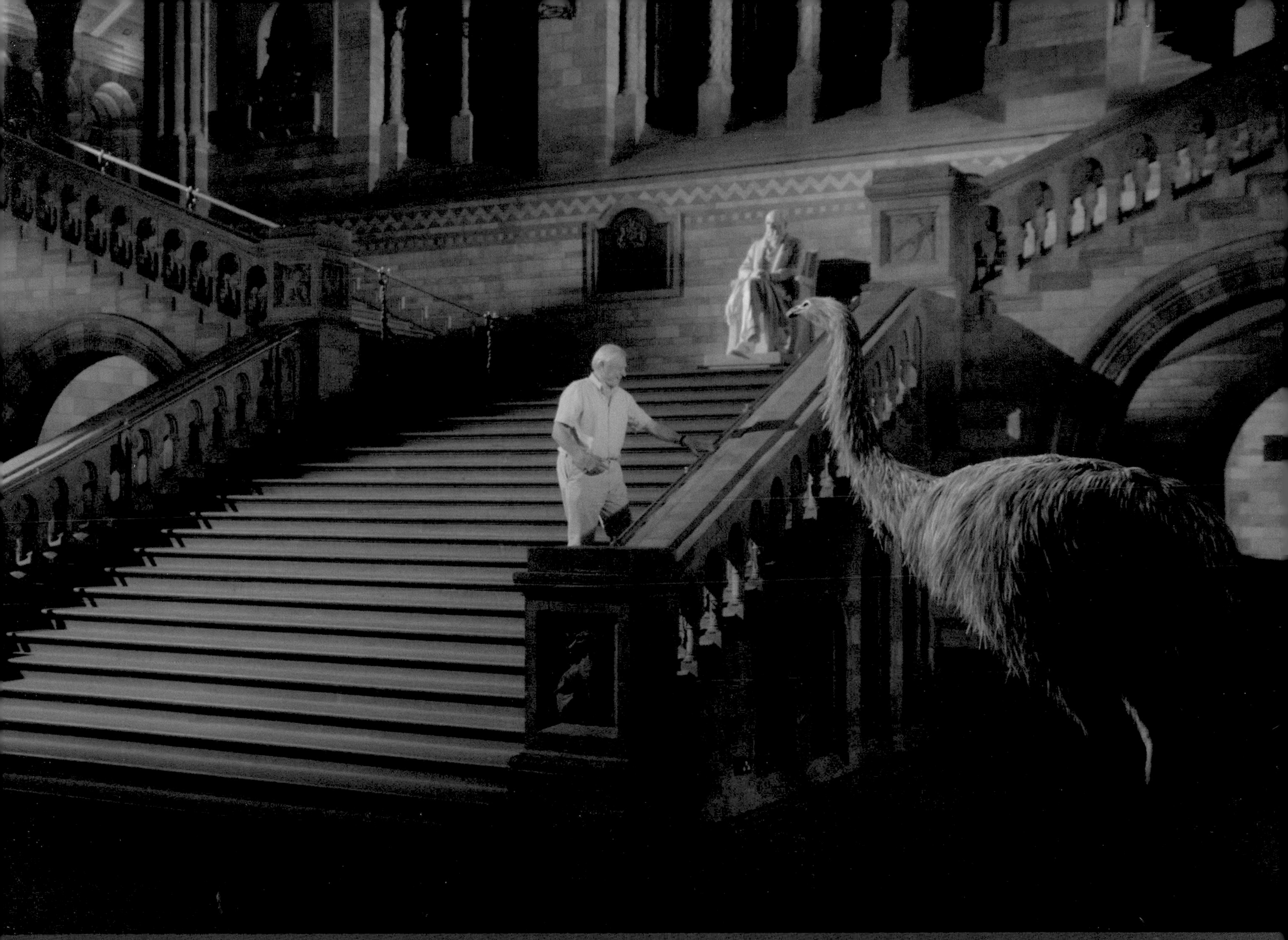

BRINGING THE CREATURES BACK TO LIFE

All these challenges were significantly increased by the project being shot in stereo 3D and delivered at ultra high resolution. The complexities of 3D and, particularly, the integration of CGI elements into these native live action backplates made this even more difficult. We had to gather detailed measurements and lighting references on set for every take. The interaction between David and the creatures, which of course weren't really there, required detailed planning, storyboarding, pre-visualisation and execution. Props for the creatures' scale and movements were used in the scene for framing, lighting and, most importantly, to ensure the accuracy of David's eyeline. Fortunately David was a superb actor – a skill he seems to have discovered quite late in life. Though sixty years of coming face to face with real animals in the wild must have been excellent practice!

The realisation of these creatures, in terms of their form, animation, rendering and compositing, will hopefully raise the bar for photo-realism and ensure these become the definitive depiction of these extraordinary lost animals. The final result of David Attenborough, in the stunning, cathedral-like Natural History Museum, interacting with them for the first time, is truly magical to behold.

Mike Davis
Supervising Producer, Colossus Productions

DIPLODOCUS
Diplodocus carnegii

ARCHAEOPTERYX
Archaeopteryx lithographica

IGUANODON
Iguanodon bernissartensis

Timeline Of Life

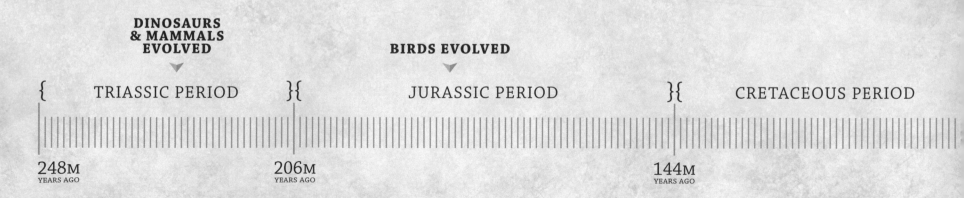

**DINOSAURS
& MAMMALS
EVOLVED**

BIRDS EVOLVED

{ TRIASSIC PERIOD }{ JURASSIC PERIOD }{ CRETACEOUS PERIOD

248м
YEARS AGO

206м
YEARS AGO

144м
YEARS AGO